YOUR
PERSONALiTY,
YOUR
HEALTH

D0973914

Other Hay House Titles of Related Interest

BOOKS

CHAKRA CLEARING: *Awakening Your Spiritual Power to Know and Heal,*
by Doreen Virtue, Ph.D. (available November 1998)

GET OUT OF YOUR OWN WAY! *Escape from Mind Traps,*
by Tom Rusk, M.D.

INSTEAD OF THERAPY: *Help Yourself Change and Change the
Help You're Getting,* by Tom Rusk, M.D.

RECREATING YOUR SELF: *How You Can Become the Person You Want to Be,
Living the Life You Desire,* by Christopher Stone

AUDIOS

AUTHENTIC POWER: *Aligning Personality with Soul,*
by Gary Zukav, with Michael Toms

CHAKRA CLEARING: *Awakening Your Spiritual Power to Know and Heal,*
by Doreen Virtue, Ph.D.

DISCOVERING AND RECOVERING YOUR CREATIVE SELF,
by Julia Cameron and Mark Bryan

PSYCHIC AND INTUITIVE HEALING,
by Barbara Brennan, Rosalyn Bruyere, and Judith Orloff, M.D.,
with Michael Toms

🐝 🐝 🐝

(All of the above are available at your local bookstore,
or may be ordered by calling Hay House at 800-654-5126.)

Please visit the Hay House Website at: **www.hayhouse.com**

YOUR PERSONALITY, YOUR HEALTH

Connecting Personality with
the Human Energy System,
Chakras, and Wellness

CAROL RITBERGER, PH.D.

Hay House, Inc.
Carlsbad, CA

HAY
HOUSE

Copyright © 1998 by Carol Ritberger

Published and distributed in the United States by:
Hay House, Inc., P.O. Box 5100, Carlsbad, CA 92018-5100
(800) 654-5126 • (800) 650-5115 (fax)

Edited by: Jill Kramer   *Designed by:* Wendy Lutge

All rights reserved. No part of this book may be reproduced by any mechanical, photographic, or electronic process, or in the form of a phonographic recording; nor may it be stored in a retrieval system, transmitted, or otherwise be copied for public or private use—other than for "fair use" as brief quotations embodied in articles and reviews without prior written permission of the publisher.

Note: The information in this book is not meant to be a substitute for medical care. Medical intuition does not diagnose illness, nor does it prescribe specific medical treatment. It is not psychotherapy. If you have a medical problem, see your physician or other licensed practitioner in your area. Medical decision making should only occur when you are in this type of trusting partnership.

Human vulnerability to disease cannot be reduced to a single physical or emotional cause. There are many genetic, nutritional, environmental, emotional and other unknown reasons why people suffer from illness and disease. Although many studies will be cited in this book that discuss specific emotional factors that contribute to illness, no study is perfect. There are limitations to any scientific inquiry. Each individual, together with one's health-care practitioner, must examine for oneself which of the various elements in one's life contribute to health or disease.

The medical intuitive readings presented in this book are composites of several similar readings. None represents a single identifiable individual. Sexes have been switched frequently, unusual names have been created, and locations have been changed. Any similarity to your name or identity is coincidental.

In the event you use any of the information in this book for yourself, which is your constitutional right, the author and the publisher assume no responsibility for your actions.

Library of Congress Cataloging-in-Publication Data

Ritberger, Carol.
      Your personality, your health : connecting personality with the
human energy system, chakras, and wellness / Carol Ritberger.
         p. cm.
      Includes bibliographical references.
      ISBN 1-56170-538-1 (pbk.)
      1. Aura. 2. Chakras. 3. Color—Psychic aspects. 4. Personality—
Miscellanea. I. Title.
BF1389.A8R58 1998
131—dc21   98-11819
                                            CIP

ISBN 1-56170-538-1

01 00 99 98   4 3 2 1
First Printing, September 1998

Printed in the United States of America

To Stephanie Noelle Franke,
Grandma's Angel Baby
January 16, 1995–January 22, 1995.
You taught me more about love in your six short
days than I had learned in my entire lifetime.

CONTENTS

PREFACE

I am a theologian with a Ph.D. in religious philosophy, and an avid student of personality behavior. In 1981, a near-death experience changed my life forever. It altered my vision in such a way that I am able to literally "see" the *aura*, the human energy system. For many years I resisted using my sight and chose the corporate world instead. That arena was safe, logical, and predictable.

My consulting business, providing corporate training through the understanding of personality types, was the foundation I used in order to teach team building and effective communication workshops. It was not until December 1995 that I felt I had enough education and experience to follow my path as a medical intuitive and to honor the work that I believe I am here to do. That work is assisting others in understanding how personality—as well as emotional, psychological, and spiritual energy—can create wellness, or lie at the root of illness, disease, and life crises.

As we approach the 21st century, the Aquarian Age, it has become clear that a dynamic change is beginning to take place in the human energy system. We are becoming more vibrant, more radiant, and more empowered. A new energy force is emerging, and that force is illuminating a whole new dimension of our persona. The energy found within this new force is nudging, pushing, and driving us toward self-exploration and spiritual awakening. It is fueling the desire to better understand ourselves, and is assisting us in learning how to get in touch with our deeper inner selves. It is helping us to remember who we really are, and that we each have something unique to contribute to life. Its energy encourages us to go within and reacquaint ourselves with the part of us that we call spirit—the part that is childlike, serving as our perpetual optimist, desiring to learn, and containing within it the power to heal.

This new energy force is influencing our thinking and affecting our behavior. We are being reminded that we alone are responsible for the direction of our lives and our health. We are being encouraged to learn to love ourselves and to become more compassionate toward others. We are being drawn toward a divine source that inspires us to look beyond the obvious and unlock the mysteries hidden within our subconscious minds—the mysteries that hold within them the wisdom to teach us how to create balance between body, mind, and spirit. That balance is necessary if we are to heal ourselves and sustain good health.

The human energy system is an electromagnetic energy force that dances with light and colors and is rich in biological and biographical information. It serves as a holographic image that reflects our state of well-being—spiritually, emotionally, mentally, and physically. Its light and colors tell the story of who we are, how we think, why we act the way we do, how our personalities affect our lives, and the state of our physical condition. Its subtle energy reveals the essence of our true selves, and its patterns and colors create a mosaic of our souls. It holds within it the keys to unlock the potential that we each hold inside.

Your Personality, Your Health is unique in its subject matter and the manner in which it connects the human energy system with predictable behavioral patterns dictated by our personalities. It offers a variety of perspectives to enable us to better understand ourselves, why we become ill, and where in our physical bodies we are most susceptible to creating illness. Viewing ourselves through the perspectives contained within this book may initiate the beginning of an empowerment process that could directly affect our lives and our health.

Your Personality, Your Health encourages and supports you to change the thoughts, emotions, and habits you believe are holding you back, to accept yourself for who you are, to embrace the innate creativity and wisdom you hold inside, and to learn to love the uniqueness you bring to this world. It offers you the opportunity to discover the vast, untapped riches that lie within you and within your divine essence. I believe you will find the rewards to be many and the effort to be justified.

🦋 🦋 🦋

ACKNOWLEDGMENTS

This book is the culmination of the enthusiastic encouragement and support that I received from many special people in my life. Each one I consider to be a major milepost in my journey. I am truly blessed by their love and want to extend to them my deepest thanks. Without that caring, I would not have had the courage to restart the work on my sacred contract or to have written this book. You are each so special, and true gifts to me from God.

I am especially grateful to my best friend and husband, Bruce. Your gentle, supportive nature has always been the wind beneath my wings. Your love and encouragement made it easier to walk the path that has changed the course of both of our lives. I thank you for your willingness to read and reread the contents of this book to add clarity and logic and for taking on additional business and personal tasks to allow me time to write. I love you more than words can express.

Diana Haas, you are the light of my life. When I asked for a child, I was blessed with you. I am convinced you are an angel in training. Your light is full of determination and the desire to make a difference. The world is a better place because of you.

My deepest love and appreciation to my family: my mother, Eunice Biano, who always listens and believes in me; and to my dad, P. G. Biano, who taught me to strive to be the best and to always give back to others; my sister, Ginger Tharp, who kept saying, "Sis, follow your dreams and don't let anything stop you"; and my brother, Petty Biano, who knows how to play and enjoy life. We could all learn more from you.

Cynthia Franke, you made my life richer when you became a part of it. I thank you for your cheerleading and for spreading the message of my work. Brian Ritberger, you are a computer whiz extraordinaire. You were always there when I had those emotional conversations with my computer, and you just jumped in and made it do what it should. When I married your father, I was blessed with the two of you.

Danny Levin, you are one of those rare, precious gifts that the universe gives us just when the time is right. Thank you for believing so much in my work that you opened the doors that led to the publishing of this book. You will always have a special place in my heart. Karin Levin, heaven is fortunate to be graced with your presence.

My heartfelt thanks to my special friends: Gayle Dax; Kelli Erickson; Jan and Dick Bowman; Christina Redfern; Melinie DiLuc; Joan Derbyshire; Rebekah Buckles; "Biz" Sherman; those wonderful, dynamic sisters, Patricia McGuire and Teri Donnelly; Marilyn, Judie, and John Marquis at John's Country Wood; Cathy Stonefelt; Brenda Burton; and Carol Rustigan. Thanks for always being there for me and believing in me. I cherish each of you deeply.

My sincerest thanks and gratitude to all who shared your energy and light with me in our sessions. Each of you were my teachers and contributed more than you will ever know to my personal growth and to the contents of this book. When our sessions were over, I would sit there and marvel at what I learned from you. I give thanks for being fortunate enough to have met you.

Thank you, Reid Tracy, Hay House vice president, for being supportive and instrumental in guiding the direction of this book. A very special thanks to my editor, Jill Kramer. Your feedback was invaluable, and your editing talents fine-tuned this book to bring cohesiveness to it. Also thanks to each of you at Hay House for adding your own special touches and input: Christy Salinas, Barbara Bouse, Kristina Reece, Wendy Lutge, and Jeannie Liberati.

My deepest gratitude to Louise L. Hay, whose book *You Can Heal Your Life* literally fell off my bookshelf one day when I was searching madly for a book that could provide a sense of direction. As I reread your book, I thought to myself that if I ever wrote a book myself, I would want your company to publish it. This book is proof that wishes *can* come true.

🔏 🔏 🔏

INTRODUCTION

This book is about *you*. It is about looking at yourself through a different set of eyes. It helps you explore the true essence of who you are, why you think the way you do, and how your health and wellness are affected as a result.

Each day presents you with a whole new set of opportunities to grow. These opportunities come wrapped in that package called life. If you view life from just one perspective, that which is familiar and comfortable, and resist looking beyond, then you miss much of the richness that life has to offer.

Your Personality, Your Health presents the concept that your personality affects more than your relationships with others. Your decision-making process, which is hard-wired or fixed in your brain, determines from the day of birth how you will interact with everything and everyone in your world, and it significantly impacts your health and wellness. Those hard-wired traits of your personality differentiate one of four specific personality types that are identified in this book by the colors of *red*, *orange*, *yellow*, and *green*. Each color denotes a personality type, which is seen as a predominant color within the human energy system, and each connects directly to a chakra.

The chakras, wheels of light, are the spiritual energy centers of the body and are responsible for the creation and regulation of the human energy system. The physical chakras, seven in number, are energetically tied to the seven endocrine glands of the body. The four chakras found in the torso of the body are associated with the physical self, and the three chakras found in the neck and head are associated with the spiritual self. Each of the four lower chakras contain "weak sites" that define the body's inclination to incur specific ailments or illnesses. The four colors *red*, *orange*, *yellow*, and *green* that are used to identify personality type align with the colors of the four lower chakras: *red*, *orange*, *yellow*, and *green*. They were not randomly selected. Chakras will be discussed in detail in Part IV of this book; however, a chart depicting the seven chakras immediately follows this introduction.

As you follow the narrative in the book, you will understand how I was impacted by three profound experiences in my life. Those experiences started me on the journey that took me from being a skeptic to becoming a medical intuitive over a period of 17 tumultuous years.

In an early part of my life, I received a "gift" that I did not ask for, did not want, and was afraid to use. My training and education was in the area of personality typology. Professionally, I conducted workshops and seminars nationally to help my clients better understand how the four basic personality types interact with each other and to impact productivity. As my vision became altered and I began seeing rainbows of color (that were eventually identified as human auras) around people, I feared a negative impact on my professional credibility should my clients hear that I was on the edge of becoming "New Age."

The death of a grandchild in early 1995 became a milestone in altering my life's purpose. I opted to redirect my entire focus to combine an extensive knowledge of personality with an ever-increasing intuitive ability to help people understand why illness occurs in their bodies and what can be done to create wellness.

After years of intensive study and research, and after working with a large number of clients providing health assessment "readings," I began to see a consistent connection between personality type and wellness or illnesses. As my work has continued, the confirmation of those observations has been reinforced many times over. Ultimately, that led to the creation of this book. Its purpose is to help you understand your personality, how you think and act, and how your personality affects your health. By opening that door, you will be better equipped to seek your personal path to wellness through whatever form of care you embrace.

As you follow the narrative and case studies, you will begin to better understand the connections between personality and wellness.

You will have the opportunity to determine your own personality color through a simplified assessment that was created to identify your decision-making processes. You can then start building the connection between your personality color and your body's weak sites. This knowledge will empower you to take charge of your state of health and wellness by providing you with a new way to look at yourself. As you understand your weak sites and their potential impact on your health, you will be better equipped to take the next steps to reach your goal of good health.

Your Personality, Your Health is laid out in four parts. Part I narrates the events that changed my life and put me on the course of evolving my medical intuitive capabilities. Part II explores the depth of information contained within the human energy system. Part III looks at personality and the important role it plays in your health and illness. This part also contains a simplified assessment so you can determine your personality color. Part IV explores the chakras in depth, and makes the connection with personality by linking the physical to the spiritual. Also, it introduces chakras 8 through 13, the ethereal chakras, and connects them to wellness and to the physical chakras, 1 through 7. Parts II, III, and IV include case studies taken from actual readings. The names, of course, have been changed to protect the privacy of the individuals.

The intention behind this work is to provide you with a wide range of information, from the basic elements of who you are and why you are, to the far-reaching impact of spirituality on the roots of your state of wellness.

Read this information. Ponder it. Discuss it. Argue it. But most of all, draw from it that which you find useful to create the life that you want and the health that you deserve.

Light and Love,

Carol Ritberger, Ph.D.
1998

The Seven Major Chakras

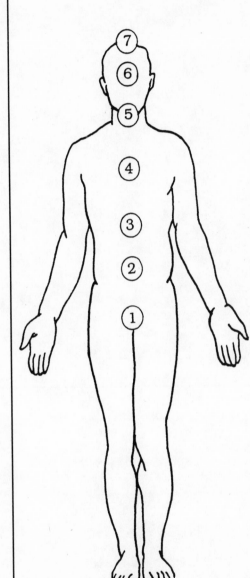

CROWN: 7th chakra
COLOR: Violet
GLAND: Pineal
Power center for connecting self with the divine

BROW: 6th chakra
COLOR: Indigo
GLAND: Pituitary
Power center for inner wisdom

THROAT: 5th chakra
COLOR: Blue
GLAND: Thyroid
Power center for self-expression

HEART: 4th chakra
COLOR: Green
GLAND: Thymus
Power center for self-love and self-esteem

SOLAR PLEXUS: 3rd chakra
COLOR: Yellow
GLAND: Adrenals
Power center for control of self

LOWER ABDOMEN: 2nd chakra
COLOR: Orange
GLAND: Pancreas
Power center for emotional control of other people

PELVIC: 1st chakra
COLOR: Red
GLAND: Reproductive glands
Power center for control of physical world

PART I

The Light of a New Dawn

Life in Transition

"If you realize that all things change,
there is nothing you will ever try to hold on to.
If you aren't afraid of dying, there is nothing you can't achieve."
— Lao Tzu

Life was simple in the late 1940s and '50s. Go to school. Care for a younger sister and brother while my mother and father worked. We moved as often as my father's business interests demanded. I assumed adult responsibility at a tender age, the result of being first-born. There was nothing in my childhood that offered an indication of anything out of the ordinary in my future. I was just another kid growing up in the baby-boom era.

As I look back on the events that altered the way I now live my life and "see" the world, I am still in awe at the synchronicity of events. Things happen when you are ready to accept them even though you may not be consciously aware of their impact on your life. Supposedly the universe does not give us more than we can handle. Unlike physical growth, spiritual growth can and often does take place when conditions seem downright hostile. What I had to learn was to accept and to trust. What I am going to tell you is a story of how my world was turned inside out by a series of bizarre events that changed my sight and my life forever.

Early in 1981, I was between consulting contracts. A friend asked me if I would like to help out in her booth at a health and beauty show. I was delighted, since it would be a pleasant way to spend some spare time. The second day of the event, I was walking the show floor looking at the displays, at the same time responding to a gut feeling that maybe there was an opportunity waiting to present itself. As I wandered around, a hand grabbed me by the shoulder from behind. I turned around and saw a small, delicate woman pulling at me. She was so frail that I thought she surely could not be the one who grabbed me. She said in near-breathless excitement that she must talk to me. She had something important to tell me and she wanted to read my palm. I politely told her, "No, thank you, I do not believe in that stuff." She was persistent in her request. Again, I rejected her invitation and told her I did not wish to talk with her. When I returned to the booth, I told my friend what had happened and how uncomfortable the situation made me feel.

Later in the day, after cautiously checking about to see whether I could spot the palm reader and wanting very much to avoid her, I decided to finish my tour of the show. This time my mother, whom I asked to keep me company, joined me. Once again out of the blue, I felt a hand on my shoulder and heard that now-familiar voice saying that she must talk with me. I turned around and heatedly said, "Leave me alone! I do not believe in what you do, and I do not want to talk to you. Go away." She persisted and volunteered that I was going to have three brushes with death in a two-week period of time, and that the third time I would have to choose whether I would go or stay. My immediate thought was, *Oh, great!* My second thought was, *What does she mean by "go or stay"?* Then I wondered, *When will these events take place?* I stood there totally shocked that this woman would twice seek me out to share such emotional information with someone she did not even know. I debated whether to respond. Should I thank her for warning me, or tell her to go frighten someone else?

The woman quickly left after giving me her message. For several minutes I simply stood there asking myself, *Now what?* Part of my education is in the field of behavioral psychology, so I am familiar with the perspective that states that an emotionally charged thought, once planted in the conscious mind, may become a reality.

This brain of ours is an extraordinary mechanism. However, it cannot tell reality from make-believe. It just acts on the information it receives. Could this be another chicken-and-egg situation? Which might come first? Will what she said come true because she predicted it or because I believed somehow it was going to happen? For the remainder of the day, I was unable to shake the feelings and fears I was experiencing. Finally, after analyzing what had happened, I decided to dismiss the whole thing. I convinced myself that the woman did not know what she was talking about. And, at best, it was clearly a case of mistaken identity. Oh, how our logical mind works with its ability to discard that which we cannot understand!

On the final day of the show, I decided to ask around about the lady who read palms to see if she had a booth. I wanted to tell her that I thought she should be more sensitive to people and their receptivity (or lack thereof) to her rantings. I also needed to ask her what she meant by the choice I would make and when these three events would happen (if any of what she said was true). I was still feeling very uneasy about all of it, and I wanted more information. Unfortunately, the woman was not to be found. Due to my uneasiness, I again asked my mother to join me.

Predictions or Coincidences?

After a long day that went well into the night, my mother and I were finally headed home. It was late, and I was both physically and emotionally drained. In that half-conscious state, I looked in the rearview mirror and saw all four lanes of the freeway filled with headlights that were fast approaching us. At first I thought it was my imagination playing tricks on me, because just a few moments before, there had been no headlights in sight. I excitedly asked my mother to look and see if she saw the headlights. She became alarmed and said fearfully, "Watch out, they're going to hit us." I assured her that they would not; however, I instinctively slowed down. As I did, the cars whisked around us so fast that it made us feel as if we were standing still. I turned to my mother and said that I had a very bad feeling that there was going to be a terrible accident. What seemed like only seconds later, there was a 16-car pileup, and six teenagers were killed. As we waited for the emergency vehicles to arrive, my mother turned to me and said, "Carol, do you think that woman was right, and this could have been number one?"

The second event took place the following week. I was having lunch with a very good friend whom I have known for years and with whom I have shared many experiences. The lunch conversation was lighthearted and fun as always. We talked about what was going on in our lives, and I told her about the strange experience that had happened the week before. As the lunch proceeded, the tone of the conversation changed. She became very upset with me and my unwillingness to accept the warning the woman had given me. As I sat listening to her growing anger, I tried very hard to remain unemotional. I felt as if I were caught up in a bad dream. I kept asking myself why this was happening. The message the woman gave me was certainly not something that should cause conflict in a longtime friendship.

I left the restaurant extremely upset and tried to rehash what had taken place. I could not understand why my friend had become so antagonistic and angry. Distracted by the events, I put my purse on top of my car to unlock the door. Not remembering that it was there, I drove away to head home. After getting on the freeway, I saw something blow off the top of my car. Instantly I remembered my purse. I pulled over to the side of the road and backed up to see if it was possible to retrieve it. It is surprising how quickly the mind works. After checking the freeway, it appeared that I had plenty of time to run out and pick up my purse and the contents that spilled out. My logic followed that I had to do this because a woman's purse contains too much of her life. Now that I look back, it was a foolish decision. However, at the time it did not seem that way. The purse landed in the middle lane. I ran out to pick it up. As I kneeled down, I heard the frightening sound of a diesel horn. When I looked up, I saw an 18-wheeler in my lane. *Oh no*, I thought, *that woman must have been wrong when she told me three. I am surely going to die now.* I realized what a deer must feel like when it is caught in the headlights. I was completely paralyzed by fear.

The next few seconds passed as if I were watching in slow motion. The truck, horn blaring, tires squealing, swerved to miss me, and its trailer hit the center divider. I could hear the crash and could smell the burning rubber from the tires as the driver fought to gain control. The wind pressure was so great that it knocked me flat against the pavement. All traffic came to a halt. As I lay there dazed and trembling, I could hear people yelling, "Crazy woman, what on earth was she trying to do? Is she dead?" Do you know how good it can be to hear people calling you crazy? I mean really hear them? That is just how I felt. I lay there thinking, *Hooray, I am not dead. Crazy, maybe, but not dead.* When I finally got up, I went to the side of the freeway and did the only ladylike thing I could do. I threw up.

For the next few days, I stayed home. I was afraid to get in the car and certainly wanted nothing to do with freeways. All I could wonder about was what number three would be like after the first two incidents. I was obsessed with fear and the thought of dying.

Now, I believe that there is much we can learn about ourselves in times of emotional turmoil. The lesson from the events that had taken place was that it forced me to reprioritize what was important and reevaluate my beliefs surrounding life and death. I had many in-depth conversations with God to try to help me understand. I was full of questions that for the first time in my life neither my education nor my logical mind could answer. I had to trust information that seemed to come from feelings and pictures that danced around in my head. I felt I was trying to understand at a different level—one that was vague, yet reassuring and comforting in its message. There was great peace within me from that new thinking.

Finally, I decided that enough was enough. I could not stay home the rest of my life trying to avoid a third incident. That evening I joined my mother and some friends for dinner at a restaurant. As we sat enjoying the food, I began to choke and had difficulty breathing. Everyone asked if I was okay, and I said yes, I just need some fresh air. I went outside. It was windy, cold, and raining, but it felt good. When

I returned, I again began to have trouble breathing. This time I could not get a full breath. I panicked and got up to leave. When I did, I must have fainted, although I felt fully conscious. As I was being taken outside, I remember hearing those around me saying how nasty it was. To me it was tranquil and warm. Instead of going to the hospital, I opted to go home. About two o'clock in the morning, I woke up fully drenched in sweat. I was burning up. Again, I could not breathe. I called to my mother to help me. All I remember saying is, "Mom, pray with me; I think I'm dying."

I cannot tell you exactly where I went for the next 18 hours, but I remember watching people work on me trying to get me to breathe. Everything in the emergency room seemed exaggerated—the lights, the smells, the loudness of the voices. It seemed that people were all yelling at the top of their lungs. I found myself above my body, looking at it with a sense of wonderment. As I seemed to float there, I turned to see what appeared to be bright lights moving toward me. For some reason I did not fear them. As the lights got closer, I could make out shapes within them. I knew that I recognized them. I felt safe in their presence and happy that they were there to keep me company as I watched what was taking place. At one point, I asked them if I was dead. I was told yes, but I could still make a choice. Here was that choice thing. If I was dead, then what choice was there?

I loved where I was. I felt free and light. There was no heaviness of being attached to the body, and I wanted to savor every feeling. There was a tremendous sense of joy and no fear. I was full of questions for my newfound light friends. I remember being told that while I was good at asking questions, I needed to listen to the answers. I was also told that I had forgotten how to look at life through the eyes of a child. They said I instinctively wanted to make it complicated and that I persistently viewed life as if it were brain surgery. My opinions and expectations of life, myself, and others were coloring my perspective. They were inhibiting my ability to move forward and to do what I had chosen to do.

I was reminded that the joy of being a child is that life is simple and fun. It is a time to be open and to learn. Every day and every thing is new. My life should be my personal candy store, filled with scrumptious goodies, and my only choice should be what I want each day. I was encouraged to laugh more. And, I was told that coloring outside the lines was OKAY. I was reminded to be present in the moment and stop focusing on the future. I never did go into the tunnel of light, nor do I remember experiencing what others tell of when they make the transition from the physical to the spirit realms. However, through the energy of my light friends, I did get to feel the presence of God and the purity of unconditional love. I look back now and realize that they came to be with me while I made the choice that would change my life.

The Choice

Suddenly, like a splash of cold water, I was jolted back to reality. I heard my daughter run into my room and call to me, "Mom, I need you to come play with me." I felt myself falling. When I opened my eyes, all I could see were bright, blinding lights. The room was full of colors. It appeared that everyone in the room had a glow about them just like my light friends. I closed my eyes and then reopened them, hoping that maybe the glow would go away. No, the lights and colors were still there. I kept asking if anyone else could see the colors. The room looked like a large prism with sunlight hitting it. The light danced, and the colors seemed to constantly change. Sometimes the colors were vivid, sometimes pale. I asked if I was hallucinating or if I had bumped my head. Was this reaction due to the drugs I'd been given or the trauma to my body? The only explanation offered was that I may have suffered some temporary vision damage because of loss of oxygen to the brain.

For the next few days as I was recuperating (the doctors told me I had probably had a severe allergic reaction to some food I'd eaten), people kept saying that I must really have some important work to do since my time was obviously not up. All I kept thinking was if they could see what I was seeing, they might not have thought that it was such a good choice. I was having terrible headaches, and the emanations of light around people never turned off. When I looked at my visitors, all I could see was a blinding glow. I had to cup my hands around my eyes in order to make out their forms. I began noticing how the colors within the glow changed from person to person. Some people were more colorful. Some people's lights stayed close to them, while others extended out several feet. I became aware that while each person's lights and colors seemed different, they each had some similarities. Their glow seemed to pulsate depending on what they were saying and how emotional they were. And, the colors I saw in each person were all pretty much the same basic hues.

Lying around gave me time to think about the bizarre events that had taken place and what I had actually experienced. It all seemed like I was living a bad dream, and none of it made any sense. I reflected back on how I felt when I was with my light friends. There were many times that I wished I was still in their presence, instead of feeling that my life was falling apart. I kept thinking about the woman at the health show who said this was going to happen. I kept hearing her say that I would have to make a choice. My mind was consumed with the need to discover what that choice really was.

One morning as I was lying in bed, I got a flash of insight and realized that my choice must have been to come back and learn how to see life through a different set of eyes. At that time, I was still unaware of how I was to use this sight to help others learn to see themselves differently. All I knew was that somehow my sight was changed, and the strange lights and colors did not seem to want to dissipate. And, curiously enough, although I could see lights around others, I could not see lights around myself.

🏵

Reflection
Messages sometimes arrive on our doorstep when least expected.
We can ignore them, dispute them, or listen to them.
Life is a series of choices. Our job is to make
the right choices at the right times.

🏵 🏵 🏵

2

A Time of Passage

*"The real voyage of discovery consists not in seeking
new landscapes but in having new eyes."*
— Marcel Proust

Two weeks after getting back on my feet, I had to fly from California to Colorado on business. I was not sure how I was going to do it since my eyesight had not returned to normal. The lights were so irritating and bright that I needed to wear sunglasses most of the time. When I went to the gate to wait for my plane, I noticed people looking at me curiously since the day was overcast and dreary. As I sat there trying to look inconspicuous, I noticed that the lights surrounding a young girl sitting near me were different than I had seen around others. This girl's lights had holes in them—holes with no light. Her colors were muted, gray, and dark. Her lights looked like the flame of a candle struggling to stay lit. I hoped she was not getting on my flight.

I was getting settled aboard when I looked up to see a woman and the young girl coming down the aisle toward me. I immediately looked away, hoping they would not stop and sit by me. I was not sure why I was feeling so uncomfortable, but the one thing I did know was that I did not want them anywhere near me. The woman asked if they could sit next to me since their seats were next to the exit door. What was I to say? I thought to myself that I would just pull out my work, ignore them, and everything would be just fine. My aloofness would surely send the message that I did not want to be friendly. A short time into the flight, the woman started talking to me. She told me that they were going to Colorado to see a specialist for her daughter. I politely listened, trying not to show too much interest. She said that her daughter had a serious blood disease, and this specialist was their last hope. The woman just needed someone to talk to.

However, knowing that this was the case did not seem to ease my discomfort. Just before we landed, the woman thanked me for listening and said that she wanted to keep in touch to tell me the results of their visit. Reluctantly, I gave her a business card. Three weeks later, I received a letter from her saying that her daughter had died. This was my first wake-up call telling me that I needed to find out more about what all of these lights and colors meant and why they were not the same in every person.

For the next year and a half, I spent time seeing psychologists, psychiatrists, optometrists, and ophthalmologists trying to find answers. Why did my sight not return to normal? No one could give me answers. Some said my imagination was running wild. Others said that the whole thing was a fabrication to gain attention. Attention! That was the last thing I wanted. I just wanted my life back the way it had been. My frustration level increased, and I grew more and more depressed. My family and friends were getting tired of me complaining about the lights. I was beginning to think that maybe I was crazy, and I could not make sense of any of it. My whole world was being turned inside out. Finally, a psychologist I had once seen called to ask me if I had ever heard of the human aura or of Edgar Cayce. I answered no to both of her questions. She then strongly encouraged me to read all I could about both. That same day, I went out and bought every book I could find about those two subjects. I look back now and thank the universe for this highly intuitive lady who finally helped me start my journey toward understanding. Another coincidence? I don't think so.

Much of what I read said that people who can see the human aura, the misty luminous glow of light and colors that follows the contour of the physical body, do so through symbolic sight. They get feelings that are conveyed into pictures. Mine were not symbolic; mine were real. If my eyes were open, the glow of light and the colors were there. They did not come and go; they never turned off. After a while, I did start to notice that my sight was changing. Instead of seeing a mist of light around people, the lights and colors were becoming more defined, with the colors focusing on different areas of the body. I became curious about what caused the changes in colors. When people were angry or stressed, it showed in specific areas of their bodies. People who were happy and optimistic had an overall glow about them. Their colors were different and bright, and their lights reached out several feet from their bodies.

I became insatiable in my need to learn and understand, and my friends and associates started asking me questions. They were curious about what I could see, and they would ask me about their colors. They wanted to know more about themselves. It seems that the information I shared with them was curiously accurate. To show them what I saw, I bought a box of crayons. I created a silhouette of the human body and began coloring what I was seeing on the silhouettes. It was as if I were doing color imaging similar to that of thermography, which is a heat-sensitive photography process where different parts of the body appear as islands surrounded by seas of vivid color. Each color meant something different. Each color as it was placed on the paper represented how and what the person was dealing with in their life. I found that the coloring added a comforting reality to what I was seeing. It seemed funny, however, that here I was in my mid-thirties and using crayons. Could this be what my light friends meant by becoming a child again? All I knew was that I had come a long way from my left-brain analytical approach to life.

Coloring Outside the Lines

I will never forget this early reading, done on a young woman sent by a friend. When this woman arrived, she apologized that she'd had to bring her daughter. It seemed that at the last minute her baby-sitter had called and cancelled. So instead of her rescheduling our appointment, she decided to bring her four-year-old with her. I thought to myself that this should not be a problem since the little girl brought her own toys and seemed very content keeping herself busy. I began the session by asking the woman what questions she would like me to answer. Once I got a feel for the direction she wanted to go, I picked up my crayons to begin coloring. Most of my coloring is outside the perimeter of the silhouette. When I did this, the little girl came over, tapped me on the leg, and asked me what I was going to do. I told her that I was going to color. She looked at me, puzzled, and said, "Aren't you kind of old to color?" I guess she was right. I suppose it did seem strange to see an adult color. I asked her if she wanted to color, too.

She said, "Oh, yes." She also said that she wished she had a box of crayons like mine. There were so many colors, and she told her mother that her pictures would be much prettier if she had my colors. I moved my box of crayons over and gave her a piece of paper with a silhouette on it. As I continued with the session, the little girl was happily coloring. She kept looking over to compare my picture with hers. When she got done with hers, she again tapped me on the leg. Did she want another silhouette? "No," she said. She just wanted to tell me that I was not very good. I found it hard not to laugh, but I asked her why. She explained, "You're not coloring between the lines." At that very moment, I remembered what my light friends had told me. *Don't worry about coloring outside the lines*. I didn't know that they meant it literally. I love it when our lessons come with a sense of humor.

Seeing Myself for the First Time

At the same time I was exploring my newfound capabilities, I was continuing my education in the psychology of personality behavior. It was not that I didn't enjoy what I could do or how it seemed to help others. It was just that my logical mind was having a difficult time dealing with it and accepting what was happening. I struggled with the feeling that I needed to learn more and to better understand what all of this meant. Deep down inside, I began to understand that there was a connection between the human aura, colors, chakras, and personality characteristics. My research and quest for understanding kept indicating that all of these factors play an important role in why people act the way they do, why they create the illnesses they do, why stress to one person is a stimulus to another, and why stress seemed to be a significant contributor to dysfunction.

It was six years into my journey when one morning I looked in the mirror and I saw lights around me. I looked at my arms and hands and was shocked that suddenly I could see my own aura. How strange it was. As I looked back in the mirror, I noticed that my aura was not a pretty sight. The colors were not vivid, but pale. There were dark colors present: gray, green, and brown. My overall light was weak, and it had spots within it that were bright red. Some areas of my body hardly contained any light at all.

I was always tired. There never seemed to be enough time to get done what I wanted to. Trying to juggle private sessions between the traveling schedule with my consulting contracts was a challenge. The private sessions had become draining. Frequently after a session, I could hardly get up. I would have to lie down just to get my physical strength back. As I looked in the mirror, I wondered why it took so long for me to see my own aura. Was this another wake-up call? Was I finally allowed to see my own aura so that I would know that I was not well? All I could think of was that young girl on the airplane and how my lights looked strangely like hers. Perhaps I too was dying. I no longer had the fear of dying as I did before; however, I thought how strange it was that my journey would end so soon. It felt like it was just beginning. I was finally starting to accept my new way of seeing the world, and opening up to how I could use this new sight in the future.

What I came to understand was that I was not dying. Rather, I was being shown something to help me learn. My own aura was showing me where there were imbalances in my body, that is, where

I had not been taking care of myself. It was showing me that all of the stress from the events over the past several years was affecting my body negatively. This created a higher awareness within me—one that I needed to share. That awareness was that while it may be easier to give to others than to take care of ourselves, caretaking must begin with ourselves if we are to have the capacity to truly nurture others.

🐦

Reflection
Growing up is not always just a physical process.
Accepting who we are and why we are here
may be our greatest growing-up challenge.

🐦 🐦 🐦

3

Validation

"The most beautiful and most profound emotion we can experience is the sensation of the mystical. It is the power of all true science."
— Albert Einstein

Looking back, it seems that the sixth year of my journey was significant in revealing how the use of my sight would evolve. The year was rich with new discoveries, new research, and new lessons—some encouraging and enlightening, others profound enough that I was forced to face many of the fears that I had hidden for so long. I discovered that if I paid attention to my own energy, I could take a pulse check on where I was emotionally and psychologically. My energy system showed me how my emotions and thoughts were creating imbalances in the flow of energy. It revealed blockages and showed me where my "stress sites" were—pointing out the resultant physical effects. While it did seem somewhat bizarre to be able to see all of this, I found it very helpful. I learned that I could strengthen my own energy in ways that would prevent me from becoming emotionally or physically drained. I found that through the awareness of my own energy, I could minimize the impact from negative people, negative emotions, and negative thoughts. I was no longer taking on the energy of others as if it were my own. Nor was I allowing others to drain me. At the same time that I was learning how to deal with my own energy, I was beginning to see similar energetic patterns of blockages in those I was working with.

My emotional comfort with my intuition continued to increase, and I was continually getting confirmations from my readings. I regularly witnessed events that validated my intuitiveness and the accuracy of my sight and insight. Yet deep down inside, I continued to doubt. I was always questioning. I was strongly skeptical regarding the accuracy of the information, and I challenged each experience until it was proven to be real. My scientific mind repeatedly wanted proof, and I found my logical self negotiating with my intuitive self. I would tell myself, *Okay, just show me one more time that what I see is real so that I can trust the validity of the information.* I started to become concerned about how I was being perceived, since my skills were associated with "psychic powers," and I have never seen myself as psychic. I was also afraid that my professional image in the business world would be jeopardized. What if it leaked out to my business clients? A straightforward, well-grounded approach to my work was critical to the success of my personality consulting business. I worked very hard to separate the two worlds in which I was living. While emotionally comfortable with the skill, deep down inside, I was reluctant to move forward with its development because I wanted to play it safe, somehow thinking that maybe I could avoid being seen as a "weirdo" or "crackpot."

Most of the readings I had been doing up to this point provided insight into how life events, emotions, and psychological issues were affecting my clients' energy systems and preventing them from creating the quality of life they desired. I was careful to stay away from illness issues and in-depth evaluations of the health of the body even though I could see where illness was occurring. I resisted this aspect of my skill because I was not yet comfortable with it. As a result of how I was interpreting the information I received in the readings, I never considered myself to be a medical intuitive such as Edgar Cayce. However, I knew that if I chose to do so, I could provide intuitive diagnoses.

Through coloring what I saw, I could offer insight into what was happening within a person's subtle energy body and their physical body. I understood that what affects one affects the other, and that all imbalances and the potential for illness start within the energy body. I began using and applying my understanding of personality to assist people in seeing how their personality traits and behavioral characteristics contributed to the responses they were experiencing. At this time in the evolution of the readings, people were more interested in why they were stuck in careers or relationships rather than in how their health was being affected. That continued to be the case until I met Jack.

Jack—Age 53

Jack specifically came to me for a reading to find out why his state of health was where it was and what he could do to improve it. He said he was always exhausted, and there were days when he hardly had the strength to get out of bed. Life seemed harsh to him, and his ability to cope with everyday tasks was becoming more difficult. He said he was afraid that his body was shutting down, and he felt like he was losing his will to live. We started out the session talking about how personality, emotions, thoughts, and relationships affect the body and our well-being. From watching his energy and how he was decoding the words I was using, I sensed immediately that the way I had been reading energy would not provide him with the information he wanted. Jack told me that he had seen a number of doctors to try to get answers. While each could assist in treating symptoms, none could clearly uncover what was causing his illnesses. He did not have a family history relating to any of the physical issues he was dealing with. He felt that there must be something deeper that was contributing to what was happening to him—some kind of blockage that was preventing him from getting better.

Jack's personality type was that of a nurturer. He was a gentle, sensitive man who needed very much to be loved and appreciated. He desperately wanted someone with whom he could share his affections—someone who would accept and love him for who he was. Jack's nature was such that he always sought the good in others. He was a humanitarian and an advocate for those less fortunate. He was not quick to judge, and he hated conflict. He would hold back from expressing his own feelings for fear that he would add to the burdens of other people. He was what one would consider a genuinely nice person.

As the reading progressed, the information that I received revealed that Jack had struggled throughout his entire life trying to get others to appreciate or like him. He had a deep fear around not being loved. He even questioned whether he was worthy of being loved. Throughout his childhood, he was criticized for not standing up like a man and for not being strong. He was chastised for his avoidance of conflict and unwillingness to fight, and he was even teased for showing his emotions too easily. His self-esteem had been severely damaged by a mother who told him over and over that he was a disappointment to her, that she wanted a son who was strong and aggressive. He constantly struggled with the fear that his mother would abandon him. To compensate for what he determined to be his lack of masculinity, Jack created behavioral patterns that allowed him to hide from his fears. He became very extroverted and took on the persona of a clown, always making fun of himself; and he discovered that in this role, others wanted to be around him.

More information kept surfacing, validating why I was seeing all of the pent-up energy in Jack's heart area. I shared with Jack that what I was seeing was a buildup of energy around his heart that was squeezing the life out of it. I told him that was where he was housing all of his frustration and anger toward himself. Jack said he hated himself for not dealing with issues, and he berated himself for not speaking up. His self-talk was toxic, destructive, and critical. As I scanned his body to see if there were any other areas being affected, my sight altered itself so that I was able to see more clearly into the physical body. It looked as if I were seeing an x-ray of his body. Until this happened, I had only seen the outside shell of the body through the energy field. It startled me. I closed my eyes and then opened them again to see if what I thought I was seeing was real. It was still there. I thought, *Oh no. Why would this be happening?* I was finally getting comfortable with the way things had been going. My intuitive skills with respect to reading and interpreting information within the energy field felt safe. I had come a long way in trusting how my sight was being used. What was I supposed to do now? How was I to explain to him what I was seeing? Information started coming faster than my mind could comprehend it.

As I traveled the inner dimension of Jack's body, I could see that some of the energy in the heart area was the result of open heart surgery. He was still in the healing process. I mentioned this to him, and he confirmed it. I continued scanning his body and found the veins in his left leg that had been removed for the heart bypass. He again validated this information. I saw red spots or signs of inflammations in his lower left calf. At first I could not tell exactly what they were, but I soon realized that they appeared to be blood clots. I quickly moved back up the body. In the neck on the right side, I found another large red spot. It appeared to be in the major neck vein. It too looked like a clot. Suddenly I got the message that he was going to have a stroke, and if he did, he would be paralyzed on the left side of his body. I asked myself, *What am I to do with this information? I'm surely not supposed to not tell him.*

This whole new sight was terribly unsettling. I had no way of validating what my intuition was telling me. Yet, I kept asking myself why I was seeing this. Was this a warning for Jack? If so, what was I to say? I started to panic. I felt myself getting sick to my stomach. I decided that the only thing I could do was recommend that he immediately go see his doctor. I chose to override my gut feeling and not tell him what I saw or what I felt. I was so relieved when the session was over, as I was extremely uncomfortable with what had happened. Now, I usually do not talk about the readings with anyone; however, in this case, I shared what I saw with my husband and told him that I got the message that Jack would have a stroke. The whole event was so distressing that I spent the rest of the day in my office with the drapes shut. I needed the time to search deep down inside and try to get answers. I did not like the new direction my sight was taking me.

A couple of weeks after the session with Jack, I received a call from a friend of his. She told me that Jack had told her about his reading and my strongly encouraging him to go see his doctor. She said she wished he had listened to me. She then proceeded to tell me that Jack had just suffered a stroke and was paralyzed on his left side. She said she thought he would appreciate hearing from me. I was speechless and confused, and angry with myself. I knew very well what my intuition had revealed. Yet, I chose not to tell Jack what I really saw. Why? Was I so afraid of the truth that I took the safe way? Did I allow my own fears to get in the way? As I look back now on that experience, I know that I would not have done anything differently.

That experience really got my attention. I said to myself, *Remind me to never again ask for proof.* This whole thing was too much for me to handle. All of the issues I had kept hidden deep inside with respect to accepting responsibility surfaced. I decided to do the only logical thing I could do: I literally took out a piece of paper and wrote a resignation letter. It read, "Dear God, I do not want to disappoint you, but you'd better find someone else for this job. I do not want the responsibility that comes from this kind of intuitive insight. Love, Carol." How naive I was to think that this would change things. I made the decision right then and there that I was not going to do any more readings, as I was afraid that a similar situation might happen again. I decided that I would commit full-time to my consulting business—at least in that area of my life I felt I had control. Enough of this use of intuition; it was too unpredictable. I had wondered for a long time whether my sight might return to normal if I didn't do readings anymore. Now was the time to test that theory. Jack died a short time later from a massive heart attack. I believe it was caused by a broken heart.

Searching for Answers

For the next seven years, I did not do any readings professionally but chose to focus my attention on research. When I was not consumed by my consulting business, I spent my time learning everything that I could about the physiology of the body and different types of illnesses. I was trying to understand why we become ill. I became active in organizations that were on the leading edge in the exploration of energy and behavioral medicine.

Psychoneuroimmunology (the study of how emotions affect the immune system) was in its infancy. I continued my own research program connecting personality with the human energy system, as I was curious about the correlation between personality and illness. I wanted to find out more about the role personality plays in how and why we create stress. There were so many questions—such as why we act the way we do, why some personality types are more prone to creating specific illnesses than others, what sort of illnesses affect each personality type, how personality expresses itself in the human energy system, the connection between personality behavioral patterns and the chakras, the emotional patterns of chakras, and the correlation between personality disorders and blockages within the energy system.

What I intuitively knew needed to be validated. I kept coming back to my original premise that personality, chakras, energy, and wellness are all somehow connected. My personality type needs to know everything humanly possible about its current interests. Consequently, the intensity with which I pursue knowledge tends to consume me—a fact my husband would gladly confirm. After a few years of intense information gathering, I felt that I had a good basic understanding of the body and the mind. However, I knew instinctively that there was something missing in the mind and body healing equation—an essential component of the formula. That component is spirit. Much of what I was studying kept suggesting that in order to truly heal ourselves, there must be a synergetic link between the body, mind, and spirit. Since I was not sure what spirit really was, I decided that was the next area to investigate.

Coming Full Circle

As the years passed, I began to miss doing readings. Research, while necessary, limited my personal interaction with people, where

I was able to connect with them intuitively. While my consulting business was prospering and demanding, it did not fulfill me, nor did it nurture my spirit. I constantly struggled with the feeling that something was missing in my life, and I began to have trouble staying focused on my consulting business. I had this nagging feeling that there was something else I should be doing. I was driven continually by a sense of urgency to move in a different direction, and I felt as if I were being pulled toward something but I did not know what it was.

In December of 1994, I woke up at 3:00 in the morning from a very vivid, disturbing dream in which my sight was taken away from me, and I was totally blind. The dream was so real that when I woke up, I was afraid to open my eyes. I lay there in the dark with my eyes closed, wondering what all of it meant. For the first time since the session with Jack, I actually feared that my sight might really go away. I recalled what had happened 13 years before and how I made the choice to return to see the world differently. How foolish of me to want it to go away. I kept hearing this voice inside telling me that it was time to go back and do readings. I tried to go back to sleep but could not. All I kept hearing in my head was: *Do your work.*

That same day, I met with a new a client, and out of the blue she told me that I had highly developed intuitive skills and must begin using them. I found this strangely curious since I had just met her. There is no way she could have known about my intuitive abilities. I guess it was time for me to hear the message, *Do your work,* one more time. That day once again changed the course of my life.

It was not until December of 1995 that I was able to finally fulfill all of my contractual obligations so I could devote myself full time to establishing a private practice. It took that entire year for me to find balance between my head and my heart so I could follow a life path that I knew would separate me from a world that I had so long functioned within. I knew in my heart that timing was everything, and the time was finally right for me to commit to using my sight to help others understand how emotional, psychological, and spiritual energy can lie at the root of illness, disease, and life crises. When I think about why it took me 14 years to come full circle, I realize that I needed to learn more about trusting myself. I had to learn through my own experiences that the ability to fully use one's intuition is directly tied into one's self-esteem. I had to be willing to surrender completely to the responsibility of being a medical intuitive—a path that I knew would change my life forever.

I am now 17 years into the journey. Every day I learn something new. I like to think of my work as a painting in progress. Every reading I do provides new information, and every day my crayons color new pictures. When I need to see how different illnesses look in the body, the universe sends me those who have similar conditions. When I need to better understand what emotional and psychological issues create specific types of illnesses, again I get multiple people with common experiences. If I find myself getting too comfortable, then a new pattern of energy or new combination of colors surfaces on the silhouettes. I realize now that the greatest lesson I have learned from all of the ups and downs on this path I have chosen is that "spirituality is a journey, not a destination." I must admit, though, that even to this day I still find myself asking why it took so long for me to finally start doing what I really came back to do. Was it that I was really slow, or did I just need the time to discover my true higher self? I choose to believe it is the latter.

❦

Reflection
Life begins not at 30, or 40, or 50, or any other calendar age.
Life begins when we realistically and honestly accept what we can
do well rather than what our self-perceptions press us to do.
In our lives, we are each given a gift. Recognizing that gift, understanding
it, and putting it to use may take a day—or may take a lifetime.

❦   ❦   ❦

PART II

A Mosaic of the Soul

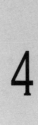

The Human Energy System

*"One cannot choose wisely for a life unless he dares
to listen to himself at each moment in life."*
— Abraham Maslow

odern science postulates that the human organism is comprised of two bodies: the visible physical body, which is made up of bones, flesh, and organs; and an invisible body that is electrical in nature. This invisible electrical body is the living energy force; it is the human energy system. The human energy system is the electromagnetic field of energy that creates the auric glow of light around a person. It has been described as a luminous radiation of light and colors that surrounds and follows the contour of the physical body. Mystics, metaphysicians, and healers have long believed that contained within the human energy system is all of the information needed to link the physical with the spiritual. S. G. J. Ouseley, in his book *Power of the Rays*, described the aura as:

> The expression of the real man....It is the sum total of his forces and emotions—physical, etheric, astral, mental, and spiritual. Concisely speaking, it is a subtle super-physical emanation surrounding a person in the form of a luminous mist or cloud. The auric emanation is the essence of a man's life—it reveals his character, emotional nature, mental caliber, state of health, and spiritual development.

29

The human energy system is pure energy in motion within the body, a composite of pulsating wavelengths. Each wavelength and its individual frequency corresponds to and represents a specific biological aspect of the physical body. Since the energy system is electrical in nature, it is constantly responding to electrochemical impulses being sent by the brain, the endocrine system, and the nervous system. It is a dynamic energy force that is continually in a state of fluctuation and change.

The human energy system is a very complex instrument, continually struggling to "stay in tune" and maintain a state of balance within its own inner structure. It is constantly adjusting and readjusting to cope with external influences. Each situation and event we experience in our lives imprints itself throughout our entire being: energetically, mentally, and physically as coded within our cells. The information we collect from our life experiences has a direct impact on the delicate balance between our energy system and the physical body. If the accumulation of information contained within the human energy system is strongly negative, then it will cause subtle energy blockages to form. These blockages clutter, clog, and restrict the natural rhythmic flow of energy. When blockages occur, then this system is not able to maintain the balance necessary to prevent the occurrence of illness. The human energy system is vulnerable to all of the same dysfunctions and illnesses as the physical body.

The human energy system has many functions, including acting as a receiver to absorb energy from the external environment and transmitting that energy and the information it contains to specific sites of the body; acting as an energetic template that allows metabolic changes to occur without losing physical structure; maintaining proper functioning of the entire body; acting as the communication link between the body, the mind, and the spirit; and assisting in the retardation and dissipation of unhealthy energetic patterns and physical invaders such as germs and disease.

In reality, the energy system is not only energy—it is energy plus information. Rich with biological and biographical information, it can tell you a great deal about yourself. Its information can provide insight into your physical, mental, emotional, and spiritual well-being. It identifies your personality traits, your behavioral characteristics, how you mentally function (how you process information and make decisions), how your mind and body electrochemically communicate with each other, your coping mechanisms, and your emotional and psychological patterns. It tells how you are dealing with current life issues.

The human energy system is a holographic image of the physical body. Consequently, what affects one will affect the other and vice versa. This energy system identifies biological "weak sites" and shows where people carry stress within their bodies, the degree that stress affects them, and where in the body a person is most susceptible to the creation of illness. The human energy system carries within it all the information needed to determine where any malfunctions are occurring, and what is needed to restore the body back to proper functioning. It is where all health and illness begins.

This system is the first to alert the mind and physical body that there is an imbalance that could potentially lead to illness. Unlike the physical body, which may create symptoms anywhere within the body, the human energy system will pinpoint precisely where the imbalance originated, the severity with which it is affecting the physical body, and the root cause of the imbalance. It does this by sending only information that is critical to creating awareness in the conscious mind, by telling the mind that something is out of sync, and then telling it where to start looking for the problem. This system operates on the principle of magnetic attraction. What you send out, you receive back. The human energy system is the law of cause and effect in its purest form.

The Impetus for Readings

People come to me for readings for a variety of reasons. Most come for health readings because they have already sensed that something is wrong. Others may be recovering from illnesses and want to update where they are in the healing process. Then there are those who have realized that something is blocking them from creating the health they want, or stopping them from getting what they want from life. They need help in identifying what is causing their blockages. Some come because they have been diagnosed with a terminal illness and just want to understand why, and learn what they can do to live the remainder of their life in a way that honors the true essence of their spirit. Many of my clients are what I call "Lightworkers." These are individuals who have a deep sense that they are here to help others prepare for the Aquarian Age. They have an inner knowingness that they are here to be the teachers, counselors, and healers of the future. Their readings focus on helping their self-remembering process and discovering their true purpose in life.

What the Human Energy System Reveals

It makes no difference why a person comes to me or in what direction the reading goes. The information contained in the human energy system communicates only the data that the person is ready to mentally and emotionally accept. The human energy system conveys this to me by directing my attention to information that is pertinent or relevant, or to the areas in the body where there are imbalances or malfunctions. It provides information in such a way that I am able to link the pieces together so I can explain what is taking place in all layers of the energy system—spiritual, emotional, mental, and physical. The human energy system tells me when using words is appropriate, when to use metaphors to get a point across, how emotionally receptive the person is to accepting the information, and when I must respect a person's defense barriers. Defense barriers are raised if individuals want to just hear information that feels safe or if they are not willing to do the work to remove their blockages. This system communicates the presence of barriers by putting up exaggerated amounts of energy in specific areas of the body.

Information is conveyed so that people can comprehend that what they are hearing is of the utmost importance. While being truthful is critical, there are times when the person is not ready to hear information in a straightforward fashion. I must take that into consideration. I do not want to add to their concerns, to create fears, or to seem insensitive. I must always honor their beliefs and attitudes. It is not my job as a medical intuitive to communicate information the way I want to, but to communicate it in a way that the person will understand. The energy activity in the brain will show me how people process information and how they decode words. Their personality type will tell me what words to use. For example, some people are literal. They want information stated in a clear, concise, and direct way. For these individuals, I must provide information in a step-by-step manner, while at the same time being careful not to make the message sound as if it is cast in concrete.

Others need to be allowed to look at all of the possibilities and to draw their own conclusions, so analogies or metaphors work best. They want information stated in a way that is visual and that allows them to see the big picture. I must choose my words carefully so that I do not imply that there is no choice involved. Then there are others who want to *feel* what I am saying, so the words I choose must be emotional in nature. For these people, I must be sensitive to my voice inflections and watch how much emotional charge is being received from the message. Each person's energy will tell me if what I am saying is registering by the activity and lights in the energy system around their head. If someone is not getting a clear message, then their energy will tell me long before their body language or words do.

Reading the Human Energy System

When I read the human energy system, I do so from two different perspectives: first, energetically, meaning that I work with the communication network of 13 chakras. (I will be discussing the seven major chakras and introducing chakras 8 through 13 in Part IV of this book.) Chakras are power centers of energy that create both the flow and structure of the human energy system. Each chakra has its own wavelike pattern and vibrational frequency and is charged either positively or negatively. These chakras and their related energetic charges are cellularly programmed to communicate with each other in such a way that they determine the overall flow of electrical currents within the physical body. Their individual and collective electrical impulses affect and regulate the biology of the body and influence psychological behavioral patterns. Next, I work with the communication network between mind and body—specifically, the endocrine glands, the major organs, and the major systems of the body.

The human energy system also contains different types of information. These different types are found within the four layers of energy that make up the energy system—they are the spiritual layer, the emotional layer, the mental layer, and the physical layer. Each layer represents a specific aspect of a person. If there is a breakdown of communication between any of these four layers, then it affects how the human energy system communicates with the physical body. The result is imbalance and the potential for illness.

Preparing for a Reading

Before I begin a reading, it is very important that I first run a diagnostic check on myself to see where I am energetically and physically. I have learned that if I am stressed, preoccupied with my own thoughts, or out of sync, then I cannot be of value to the person being read. If I detect any imbalance, then I spend time rebalancing myself. Any imbalances will inhibit the quality of information I receive.

When a person schedules a reading with me, that gives me permission to enter their energy system for the purpose of accessing information for the reading. Prior to each reading, I spend intuitive time with the person on a purely energetic level. This is where I utilize my intuition to get to know the person in their purest form. During the reading itself, I use my eyesight to validate what I pick up through my intuitive skills.

Client Readings

I would like to share some of these readings with you, to help you become aware of the depth of information contained within the human energy system. While I understand that you may not be able to see human energy (the aura), nor may you even have the desire to do so, I hope that my explanations can bring an awareness of the volumes of information that the human energy system contains. My intention in describing what a reading reveals is to spark an interest in you to learn even more about the human energy system. If nothing else, I hope that I can arouse your curiosity in such a way that you will want to know more about who you are and why you act the way you do.

If you can accept the fact that there is an energy system and that that system affects the overall well-being of the physical body, then you can begin to access its information in such a way that it can tell you where imbalances occur. You can also learn how to harness the power of the energy system to create both the health and life you want. (*Note: All names have been changed to protect the privacy of my clients.*)

Michael—Age 55

Energy analysis: Extreme overall depletion of the energy system. Suffers from physical exhaustion and shows signs of chronic fatigue. Electrical storms in head area. Mental disarray. Chemical imbalance in brain. Signs of damage to areas on the right side of the brain. Very little energy activity or light present. Erratic energy flow in both arms. More on left side. Tremors in hands. Most energy focused in upper torso area. Lower extremities show very little energy flow. Poor circulation in legs and feet. Red energy protrusion in area of brain where brain stem originates. This energy buildup is affecting motor skills, causing energy blockages in upper spine, primarily the second, third, fourth, and fifth cervical vertebrae. Signs of nerve degeneration. Severe muscle tension in shoulder area and midback. Colors indicate buildup of toxins and waste in muscle structure. Signs of depression. Color red/brown indicates central nervous system affected. His weak sites are the chest, neck, and upper shoulders (4th, 5th, and 11th chakras), and specifically the cerebrospinal nervous system.

Diagnosis: Michael was diagnosed by medical professionals with Parkinson's Disease four months after this reading.

Likely cause: Extreme unwillingness to deal with change. Lack of belief in himself. Emotional issues pertaining to low self-esteem. Lack of drive and absence of courage to go after what he wanted. He always felt he was not worthy of having what he desired. Childhood experiences and the negative emotions he attached to them affected his self-worth. He believed that his life had no meaning or purpose. He lived with the belief that it was a mistake that he was even born. There was a strong energy loss around his connection with God. This felt contradictory because Michael was raised in a very structured, strict religious belief system that should have served him well. Yet, when Michael needed God to help him the most, he felt that God abandoned him. Because of this, Michael disconnected from God. At a very young age, Michael started living his life based on an erroneous perception that he would never be able to get what he wanted. He spent his life fulfilling that mental perception. He never took the time or had the desire to reevaluate the perceptions that were limiting him. He was never able to get in touch with his true essence and discover his unique talents. He was basically disconnected from himself.

Gladys—Age 63

Energy analysis: Energy buildup and red hot spots in 2nd chakra. Red/Orange energy around pancreas. Kidneys being affected by pancreas malfunction. Deep emotional issues surfacing in all colors. Indicators of diabetes. Sugar level unstable. Thyroid area cloudy. Metabolic rate off. Extremely overweight. Red hot spots in muscles around joints. Muscle structure dense. Heavy buildup of waste in muscle structure throughout the whole body. Patterns and colors indicate fibromyalgia. I checked to see if there were signs of osteoarthritis. No definitive signs. Blood pressure high. Poor circulation in legs and feet. Inflammation in right wrist; however, the cause is more muscular than Carpal Tunnel Syndrome. Immune system weakened from viral infection in chest, throat, and sinus areas. She has a cold. Energy field is generally weak. Body showing signs of emotional and psychological imbalance. Kidneys distressed and indicate presence of stones. Sleep cycle off. When I asked her about her sleep, she said that she has not had a good night's sleep in years. Wakes up tired and has difficulty getting out of bed because of aching muscles and sore joints. Her weak site is her lower abdominal area (2nd chakra).

Diagnosis: She confirmed findings of diabetes and fibromyalgia. Also said that she suffers from kidney stones. Endocrinologist is working with her to stabilize glands and reestablish chemical balance in the body.

Likely cause: Paranoia. Believes others are out to get her. Afraid that people will take advantage of her. She feels that nobody likes her or understands her. High levels of stress in her life. No family support system. Lives alone. Fearful that she will never have enough food and money. Fears that her health will force her to have to retire early and she does not have enough money to support herself. Uses her illnesses to get other people's sympathy. Emotional energy around feeling sorry for herself. Has a slight connection with God; however, admitted that she really doesn't know whether she believes there is a God. Suffers from psychological disorder of hypochondria. Uses food as an emotional nurturer. Does not feel that she has control over her life. Blames others for everything that happens. Sees herself as a victim.

Maggie—Age 38

Energy analysis: Energy protrusion in eye area. Looks like blood flow issues to brain. Brown/red color in brow area. Brown/olive green color buildup in sinus area representing sinus congestion. Concentrated energy buildup around head. Cloudiness, indicating chemical imbalance in neurological functioning. Muscle tension in neck and shoulders. Muscle inflammation and hot spots in both shoulders; however, more right side than left. Feels like she has a headache during session. Energy block solar plexus (3rd chakra) and dark orange/red/brown streak running down entire spinal column. Stomach congestion. Showing signs of excessive accumulation of acid in stomach. The pH balance of her body is off. Adrenals overproductive in release of stress hormones. Signs of posttraumatic stress syndrome. Menstrual cycle not consistent. Signs of severe mood swings. Her weak sites are her chest, neck, and upper shoulder area. Her heart (4th chakra and 11th chakra) is energetically depleted so adrenals (3rd chakra) overstimulated to compensate for energy imbalance. Breathing shallow and rapid. Mild heart palpitation.

Diagnosis: Suffers from severe migraine headaches to the extent that some last up to seven days. Experiences blurred vision and dizziness, but her doctor could not identify why. Stomach very sensitive and has to watch diet to manage her headaches. However, headaches are really triggered more by emotional stress. Suffers from anxiety attacks. She is a very nervous person. Extremely sensitive to light and sound. She was working with a cranial sacral practitioner and hypnotherapist. Her physician had prescribed medication to help with headaches. She chose to take an alternative approach. The cranial sacral work appears to be helping tremendously.

Likely cause: Maggie found out at a very young age that if she were sick, she got more attention; and so she would fabricate illnesses. She also used her illnesses to get out of doing things that she did not want to do. She developed coping mechanisms around personal denial. She had difficulty interacting with other people. Very reclusive in behavior. When Maggie was a child, her mother always complained of headaches. Maggie said she could remember even when she was very young that when people would ask her how she felt, she would always say that she had a headache even if it were not true. She blamed getting headaches on anything that made her unhappy. She used them as a manipulative tool to get others to do what she wanted. She lived life from a fantasy perspective and was unable to see situations for what they really were. She constantly blew things out of proportion. Her body responded by suffering from severe stress attacks. She used food as punishment. If she was being what she considered bad, she would eat tremendous amounts of sugar so she could get a headache. Then there were other times she would just quit eating completely, intentionally depriving her body of the food and fuel it needed to function properly. General emotional and psychological patterns centered around self-destructive behavior. Root cause of headaches originated within the emotional layer of energy. Very low self-esteem.

Joseph—Age 43

Joseph was referred to me by a physician. At the time of the reading, he was being treated for liver inflammation. He was not showing any signs of improvement so the doctor was interested in my diagnostic evaluation. I was not aware of what he was being treated for until I actually got into the session and had him sitting in front of me. My intuition did not surface any major disturbance within the liver. The health issue was more in the thyroid gland and immune system.

Energy analysis: Severe energy protrusion in throat and neck area. Lymph nodes swollen, and presence of dark red energy extended out about seven inches from his body. General swelling in neck. Color distortion and patterns indicated the presence of cancer. Gray color indicated immune system involvement. Black color indicated cellular and tissue degeneration and probable malignant growth. When I went into the body, there was the presence of a cancerous nodule on the thyroid gland and indicators of cancer in three lymph nodes on the right side. I kept feeling a lump in my throat representing a strong energetic blockage. The overall colors within his energy system were dark orange/brown showing emotional confusion and the presence of high levels of toxins. There was some energy buildup and red color (inflammation) in the liver area. A dark gray color was predominant within all lymphatic sites of his body. Immune system showed signs of being under attack and losing the battle. There was a hot spot of red in right testicle; however, no presence of cancerous colors or patterns of energy. His colors and patterns of energy showed that his entire glandular system was in a state of crisis. Every chakra in his body was overcompensating energetically to try to regain balance. Joseph's body needed help and needed it quickly. His weak sites were his pelvic area, reproductive glands, and immune system (1st chakra). Yet, his health issues were caused from emotional stress that settled in the throat (5th chakra).

Diagnosis: I did not tell Joseph during the session that I saw thyroid cancer. It was up to his doctor to confirm my findings. I do not diagnose medically. What I did discuss with him were the emotional and psychological issues that I felt were the root cause of the problem. After the session, I spoke with his doctor and told him what I had seen. Joseph went in the next day for tests that confirmed the presence of cancer in the thyroid. Three days later, Joseph had surgery, and within five days of the surgery, his liver inflammation cleared up. I would like to emphasize that the reason the doctor did not suspect cancer was that the body was not displaying any symptoms that would have triggered that type of evaluation. However, the energy system pinpointed the precise cause of the liver problem and its inability to detoxify the body the way it needed to.

Likely cause: Joseph was the younger of two boys. His older brother seemed to do everything right. Joseph continually felt that he walked in his brother's shadow. Their relationship was very competitive, and from Joseph's perspective he would always end up the loser. Instead of competing for affection and recognition, Joseph withdrew and would not assert himself, which was contradictory to his personality type. In fact, he was always teased because he never talked. His brother would tell his friends that "the cat got Joseph's tongue." This teasing left deep emotional wounds. When frustration finally drove Joseph to find his voice, it seemed like nobody was there to hear him. He began feeling that he was inadequate and could not stand up for himself. The more frustrated he became, the more aggressive his behavior was. He started letting his fists do his talking, and used dishonesty and lying as a means of making himself seem important. He detached emotionally from life itself, bragging about how unemotional he was toward everyone and everything, and how no one would ever hurt him again. For him, emotions became a sign of weakness. His frustration with himself and with others settled in his throat area (5th chakra). After years of storing negative emotional energy in this part of his body, it finally reached a point where it could not store any more. He was surprised when I told him that his body had been sending messages of the imbalance for years. It was just that he chose not to listen. The result was a severe protrusion of energy in the throat, and that is what contributed to the creation of cancer in the thyroid gland. Joseph acknowledged his choice to hang on to his anger.

The Impact of Energy on Health

I hope that by sharing these sessions, you can better understand the valuable information contained within the human energy system. Most important, I hope that you can begin to see that when negative energy is attached to thoughts and emotions, every aspect of your being is affected: body, mind, and spirit. Negatively charged energy creates energetic blockages, and blockages create imbalances. Illness is the result of those imbalances. I believe that each of us can look at our life experiences from two different perspectives. One, we can see them as an opportunity to learn. When we do this, we create an energy that allows our true essence to flow throughout every cell in our body. The result is a perfect balance, energetically and chemically. This balance allows our inner healer to do its job. We are healthier and happier, and our lives take on a sense of purpose. Or, we can see our experiences as one-darn-thing-after-another. The result is a life full of disappointment and emotional dysfunction— one where the potential for illness looms around every experience. The choice is ours.

🦋

Reflection
Our physical bodies speak to us in a language we understand.
We eat, drink, laugh, cry, hurt, rest, move, speak and listen,
or do a number of physical things without giving them conscious effort.

Our energy systems speak to us also—in a different language.
Good health may dictate that we become multilingual,
understanding both the language of our physical bodies
and the language of our energy bodies.

🦋 🦋 🦋

5

The Language of Energy

"The life of man is a self-evolving circle, which from a ring imperceptibly small, rushes on all sides outwards to new and larger circles."
— Ralph Waldo Emerson

The human energy system is an intricate, highly developed communication network that is constantly talking to all of the other systems within your physical body. Externally, it tells others who you are, energetically, long before your words or actions do. The human energy system is the common interface through which you interact with *everything*—both inside and out. Your energy system acts as an antenna—sending, receiving, and recording the information it gathers. As this powerful communication network receives information, it transmits the data to specific areas of the body where it is stored in the cells for future reference. It records all experiences, both past and present—all thoughts, all memories, and all emotional reactions. This stored cellular memory then becomes the language link through which your energetic body and physical body communicate with each other.

The language of energy synthesizes your conscious and your subconscious mind. It communicates how your brain functioning, your perceptions, your attitudes, your beliefs, and your values are genetically hard-wired. Through its color variations, it reveals your fears, anxieties, insecurities, and emotional vulnerabilities. Thus, just as physical diseases appear as color variations, psychological issues and past traumas of all types also add colors and energetic variations to the human energy system.

Four distinct energetic layers—the spiritual layer, the emotional layer, the mental layer, and the physical layer—contain this information. Each of these four layers communicates specific information that provides insight into who you really are. The way these layers of energy interact and communicate within themselves determines how you approach life. Are you external to internal? Or internal to external? Let's begin our journey toward understanding the four layers of energy—let's uncover the volumes of information the human energy system can reveal, and what it can tell you about yourself.

The Spiritual Layer of Energy

The spiritual layer of energy is the central core and the purest representation of who you are energetically. It is your true authentic self. The wisdom communicated from this layer of energy encourages you to listen, to be introspective, and to speak only the truth of your divine self. It is what aligns you with your connection to what you call God. It is within this layer that you house your deepest feelings around what you believe. Your spiritual energy assists you in making the choices in life that will be in your highest good; its energy encourages you to seek the path of higher consciousness. It is within this layer of energy that you find meaning and purpose in your life, and it is through this energetic portal that you access all of your talents and unique qualities. When you approach life from your spiritual perspective, there are no boundaries. There are no shoulds or should nots, no rights or wrongs, no good or bad. Everything just "is." Spiritual energy sees every experience as a lesson and every lesson as an opportunity to grow. The rewards that you reap when you maintain balance within this layer of energy are many. Good health is one of them.

When I connect with the spiritual layer of a person, I ask to access different kinds of information. First, I want to meet their inner child. I am not referring to the emotional inner child that psychologists talk about that becomes wounded from life's experiences—I find that inner child in the emotional layer of energy. What I am referring to is the inner child that represents the deepest, purest essence of who we are; the inner child that always remains innocent and naive and never becomes cynical or jaded. Think of this inner child as a two-year-old who sees each day as something new to experience and an opportunity to learn. It is through these eyes that we sustain an awe of life. It reminds us to open our eyes to beauty and kindness—everything this inner child sees is viewed through love. It allows us to touch the farthest reaches of our imagination. It has no expectations. Life is basic and simple. It is in the spiritual layer of energy that I experience a person's sense of humor. I begin to understand what truly brings someone joy. While our lives may be filled with trauma and dysfunction, I have come to an awareness that, no matter what has happened in a person's life, at their purest level of spirit, their spiritual inner child remains optimistic and hopeful. These emotions contribute substantially to our ability to heal.

Next, I ask if I may access a person's belief system around what they call God. I am using the word *God* because it is universally used and understood. However, it really makes no difference what a person calls their God, nor does it matter if their God is male or female or if it has a particular religious denomination attached to it. What does matter, however, is that there is the presence of a strong divine belief system. The value of having such a system is that it brings a sense of comfort and joy into our lives. It allows us to open up and get to know ourselves in a deeper, more intimate way. Our relationship with our divine belief system is the most important factor in the healing equation. It is what adds life and energy to our spirit. It is what connects us with our emotional, mental, and physical self. People who do not have a strong divine belief system find it more difficult to heal or to cope with the challenges that life throws their way.

I then get a sense of how a person talks to God. Prayer, whether formal or informal, is an important part of how we heal. By dialoguing daily with God, we create a synergistic alignment between the body, mind, and spirit. When we pray, we bring into being unified healing patterns of energy from our spiritual and emotional layers that are communicated to our mental and physical layers. Over the course of my practice, I have seen and experienced the power of prayer. I have learned that when we face difficult challenges, especially those around our own health or the health of those we love, prayer is a powerful healer. Through prayer, we surrender our fears and our burdens to God. Through prayer, we turn the energy of fear, which is frenzied and antagonistic, into the energy of love, which is congruent and harmonious. We quit trying so hard to be in control. We allow ourselves to let go. This tells the body that it can go back into a natural state of energetic balance so it can create the perfect physical environment for healing to occur. Through prayer, we solicit the help of our inner healer/physician—that inner physician called our immune system. When we release ourselves to God, we give the body permission to return to its natural rhythmic patterns. We change the chemistry of the body so the immune system can do its job.

Inherent within each of us is the power to self-heal. In fact, every cell that makes up our physical body has been preprogrammed with an innate intelligence that responds to the natural impulse to heal. In other words, no matter how severe any malfunction is within the body, it will always seek wellness over illness. Yet, given our power to heal, it remains a mystery why the miracle of true healing is not an everyday occurrence. Perhaps the objective to heal is so simple that we have forgotten how. Maybe we just have to stop preventing the body from doing its job by hanging on to our fears or emotional wounds—that is, we just have to "let go and let God." Perhaps we have to let the energy of love work its miracles.

Sacred Contracts

The spiritual layer also contains information around our sacred contract with our God. It is the things-to-do list for this lifetime, a contract that we make prior to being born. While I do not get to see everything on a person's list, I do get a sense of their primary objectives. For example, say a person's objective is to work on emotional issues surrounding abandonment. In this lifetime, that person will have the opportunity to create relationships that allow them to work through that issue. They will either create relationships that are emotionally fulfilling, trusting, loving, and have a sense of longevity, or they will continually put themselves in relationships where the outcome will most likely end in the feeling of being abandoned.

If a person chooses the latter, then they will enable themselves to stay emotionally wounded. Their fear surrounding abandonment will become a self-fulfilling prophecy. They will perpetually see themselves as victims and consequently attract others who will want to control them, who will feel sorry for them, who will enable them to stay wounded, or who will eventually leave them. While it is true that we have choices in every aspect of our lives, if we do not choose things that move us toward a deeper understanding of ourselves or toward our higher self, then we are not honoring our contract. (By the way, I have learned that allowing ourselves to stay wounded is not an option we can exercise if we want to fulfill our contract or stay healthy.)

How do you know when you are not honoring yourself or your contract? Look for patterns of behavior that do not serve you well—pay attention to how you are living your life. Listen to your self-talk. Ask yourself if your life is flowing smoothly or if you feel as if you are running an obstacle course. Listen to your body. It will tell you when you are making the choices that are not in your best and highest interest by providing warning signs. It will alert you by creating dysfunction in specific areas of the body where you are holding on to old emotional wounds. If you remember that the number-one item on your sacred contract is to learn and to teach others, then it will help you in remembering what you need to do to fulfill your contract. As the cliché states, you can either see your life as a glass half-empty or half-full. Life is one choice after another. It is the opportunity for you to learn and grow. If you are to teach others, then you can only do so by walking your talk. You must do it by learning from your experiences and not allowing yourself to remain emotionally wounded—and, by checking things off your to-do list.

The Emotional Layer of Energy

Once I have an understanding of where the person I am reading is on their spiritual layer, I then explore their emotional layer. The emotional layer also contains a wealth of information. First and foremost, it contains the person's life history from both their past lives and current life.

Before I go into detail about past-life information, I feel I must first tell you that because of my early religious training, I did not for most of my life believe in reincarnation. However, since working with past-life concepts, I have changed my thinking. I have done too many readings on people who could not identify why they experienced deep-seated fears and extreme behavioral patterns at a very early age, who then found their answers through exploring their past lives. I have also read people who had spent years in therapy, only to be told that their real fears must be originating at a much deeper level, perhaps from previous lifetimes. While past-life information is not something that can be scientifically validated, I have watched people react to past-life information in such a way that it finally provides them with answers to questions that have been haunting them for most of their lives. I have also worked with past-life regression therapists who have assisted people in making major breakthroughs with respect to issues that have blocked them for years.

Sherry—Age 38

To give you an idea of how past-life issues can affect a person in their current life, I would like to share the reading I did with Sherry. When I began the session, I started out by telling her that I had the opportunity to see two of her past lives, and if she was interested, I would share that information with her. She said she was very interested. I then went on to tell her that these two lifetimes had strong emotional energy around them and that I thought they might be affecting her current life. In both of these lifetimes, she died by drowning.

The first was an ancient Egyptian lifetime where she fell into a river while getting water. She did not know how to swim and found herself going deeper and deeper underwater. The river was muddy and dark, and she struggled to right herself so she could return to the surface to catch her breath. She was unsuccessful, and drowned. In the second lifetime, she was crossing the English Channel by ship in a fierce winter storm. She was afraid, and hid in a closet, thinking she'd be safe there. As the ship began to capsize, she struggled to get out of the closet but was pinned in. Again she drowned.

As I shared this information, Sherry started sobbing. I watched her release waves of emotional energy. She said that I had finally explained why she had such a fear of water or of not being able to breathe. As far back in her childhood as she could remember, she suffered from panic attacks whenever she got near water or if she felt she could not get her breath. She told me that at age four, her mother had decided that Sherry needed to learn to swim. She had become so violently ill that she'd had to be taken to the hospital. No one, not even the doctor, had been able to explain what caused the violent illness.

She also shared that she has always had a fear of boats and suffered from claustrophobia. She recalled as a child that she and her family had gone to a fair, and her sister wanted her to ride the little boats with her. Sherry resisted, but her parents forced her to go. She screamed at the top of her lungs the whole time. She never understood where these fears came from because she tried very hard to avoid anything in her current life that would have somehow aroused them.

Finally, Sherry seemed to have information that her conscious mind could accept, which confirmed why she held those fears. Sherry called me several months after our reading to thank me and to tell me that she had just gotten back from a wonderful week-long cruise. Can you believe it? She said that she had not realized how much these fears had affected her or how much they had prevented her from enjoying life. She said that she was still working on overcoming other fears and making good progress because she understood them. It was Sun Yat-Sen, first president of the Provisional Chinese Republic, who expressed this so eloquently when he said, "To understand is hard. Once one understands, action is easy." How true this is.

Past-Life Information—a Paradox

Past-life information can be difficult for many people to accept because it cannot be validated. When past-life data is brought forward from our subconscious mind into our present consciousness, we are asking our conscious (linear thinking) mind to accept information that has, for it, no basis. Past-life information confuses the conscious mind because it cannot match a current-life memory, experience, thought, or emotional reaction to the information that it is being asked to accept. When our conscious mind becomes confused, it mentally short-circuits, which lessens the ability to think clearly. So, rather than staying confused, the mind takes the path of least resistance, and determines that the past-life information it is being asked to process is not usable; it is dismissed. Dismissing may work for a while, but if the subconscious mind determines that it is important for a memory from a previous life to surface in order to help one understand current fears and issues, then it will become more persistent in bringing forth the awareness. The subconscious mind will continue to press the conscious mind to accept the validity of the data. The connection will eventually take place because the subconscious mind will attach an emotional reaction to the information. When this occurs, then the conscious mind can accept it and will store the information away for future use.

Another reason that past-life information can be difficult for the conscious mind to accept is because of the way it reveals itself. Past-life information usually emerges through dreams, through a vague recollection, or through some kind of strong emotional reaction. Past-life data is encoded deep within the psyche. For one to access the memories of past lives requires that the person either be asleep or be sufficiently skilled to reach a state of deep relaxation. Everyone has the ability to tap into their own past-life memories (8th chakra); however, if a person lacks the ability to attain the necessary state of relax-ation, then it can turn into a frustrating process. Should you become interested in exploring your past lives, but do not feel you are skilled enough to prepare yourself, then I would suggest seeking the services of a hypnotherapist. Most hypnotherapists are trained in past-life regression. They know how to prepare a person to facilitate the elici-tation of information in a way that is comfortable and feels safe.

Current-Life Information

When I have finished gathering a person's past-life information, I start connecting it with the person's current-life biography. I find that current-life data is both easier to access, because there are usu-ally stronger emotional charges attached to it, and also easier to communicate, because of the person's ability to readily recall it. As I review the person's life, working from their current age back to their birth, I look for situations—traumatic life events or life-altering experiences—that would cause any severe emotional wounds or deep fears. I want to know if their divine belief system served them well in these times. Or did they turn away from their God? If so, have they reconnected? I look for other kinds of residual dysfunctions they are carrying over from their life experiences. Are they holding on to old traumas? Are they willingly preventing themselves from moving for-ward? Are they using their emotional wounds to manipulate others to get what they want? Do they wear their emotional wounds as if they are badges of honor? A yes answer to any of these questions has a long-lasting impact on our health and how we heal. The stronger the negative emotional reaction to our life experiences or the hard-er we resist letting go of our fears, emotional wounds, and dysfunc-tions, the more difficult it will be for us to have either the life or health we want. Now, I do not mean to make light of the traumas that we each have endured. However, if we are to truly heal, then we must face our fears, wounds, traumas, and dysfunctions in such a way that we change the emotional energy attached to them.

I use the story of *The Wizard of Oz* as a way to put our fears into proper perspective. When we decide to face our fears, we are very much like Dorothy, who, when she entered the great castle of the wizard, heard a loud, strong, aggressive voice say, "What do you want?" Her first reaction, similar to our own, was to say, "Oh, nothing. I must be in the wrong place." It is too frightening to speak up and ask for what we want. It is even more frightening to face the fears that we have so carefully hidden for all our lives. If you could just remember that your fears are not as big as they seem, but in actuality, are just like the Wizard. Visualize an unimposing guy standing on a box speaking into a big microphone and amplifier trying to make himself appear omnipotent. When you see your fears for what they really are, they lose their power over you. I also have found that a sense of humor is a wonderful healer and can help put our fears into a manageable perspective.

Expectations—Ours and Others

How we deal with expectations is another factor that affects the delicate balance of energy in our emotional layer. I find that people who live their lives based upon an expectation that others will fulfill their emotional needs, or will be responsible for bolstering their self-esteem, consistently set themselves up for emotional disappointment. If people choose to live with expectations that they really have no control over, they will always feel emotionally trapped. They are prevented from learning how to nurture themselves, and continually feel emotionally starved. The result is that they set themselves up to remain wounded. They become stagnant in their personal growth because they choose not to accept responsibility for it. Stagnation has strong negative emotional charges attached to it. Those negative emotional charges create an energetic discord within our spirit that prevents us from fulfilling our sacred contract. It creates congestion and blockage in all layers of our energy field, which disrupts the healthy functioning of our physical body.

Forgiveness Is Not Easy

The emotional layer of energy also reveals a person's capacity to forgive—forgiveness first of self and then of others. In many readings, I find that illness has manifested in the physical body because people are still holding on to old emotional hurts. They have not learned how to let go and forgive.

Karen—Age 45

Let me give you an example of this inability to forgive by sharing a reading I did with Karen, the eldest of five children. As far back into her childhood as she could remember, her mother was always sick and complained constantly of being too tired to do anything. Her mother suffered from chronic depression and severe mood swings. Consequently, she relied heavily on Karen for emotional support and for taking care of her and the others within the family. Karen became the target of her mother's emotional outbursts at a very early age, as she was expected to be a role model for her siblings. When she did as she was told, her mother praised her. However, because she had no control over her mother's mood swings, most of the time Karen's life at home was untenable. Karen could not wait for the day when she could move out and get on with her life.

The problem was that Karen could never get far enough away from her mother. Then as life dealt its cards, Karen's mother needed to be sent to a convalescent hospital for care. Her mother was adamant that the hospital be somewhere close to where Karen lived. Reluctantly, Karen agreed. Whenever Karen went to visit her mother, it was the same thing as when she was young. Her mother yelled at her and made her feel guilty for not wanting to take care of her. She told Karen that she was self-centered and cruel for not coming to visit her more often. One day the hospital called and told Karen that she had to come and take her mother to another facility because they were not able to deal with her. Karen finally reached her wit's end. She went to see her mother and proceeded to unleash all of the hate and anger that she had pent up inside for so long. Her outburst shocked her mother and caused her to go into cardiac arrest. Her mother died the next day. When I asked Karen about her reaction to her mother's death, she said that finally she had some peace. I asked her if she'd ever worked on trying to forgive her mother. She said, "Why should I? The woman hurt me and ruined my life. I am never going to forgive her."

When I did the reading on Karen, her mother had been dead for eight years. Yet, when I went into Karen's emotional layer of energy, it was as if her mother's death had just happened 30 days earlier. She was still carrying that much emotionally charged energy around it. For most of her life, Karen has hung on to the negative energy of hating, rather than releasing it by working on forgiveness—or at least letting go of it. In fact, her bitterness and anger toward her mother had been so strong throughout her life that it even colored her relationship with her own children. When I asked her about this, she said that her kids tell her all the time that she is just like Grandma. The price Karen has paid for not forgiving is that her hatred has been sucking the life out of her. She stored her hate in her "weak site"— in her chest area. She was disappointed and disillusioned that her own mother would hurt her so deeply.

Now I should tell you that the reason Karen came to see me was because she had been diagnosed with breast cancer. She wanted to get a better understanding of why something like this would happen to her since there was no family history of cancer. I bet you can guess what I said. I suggested that she most likely developed breast cancer because she had hung on to the anger around her mother for so long, rather than releasing it and learning to forgive first herself and then her mother. Even with her mother dead, Karen was living each day energetically as if her mother were still alive draining her of energy. That is a pretty high price to pay for not forgiving.

I have read many people who after years are still carrying around the old baggage of an emotional hurt that could have been unloaded long ago if they had just practiced forgiveness. I understand that forgiveness is not easy and can be a very painful process. I also understand that each one of us has our own beliefs and boundaries around how we forgive. Here is where a person's personality type starts to reveal itself. Some personality types do not feel they can forgive until the other person gets what they deserve. It is that old "eye-for-an-eye" belief. Other personality types feel that justice must be served before they can forgive. These people will personally take it upon themselves to be sure that the person they are forgiving realizes without a doubt what they have done and how hard it is to forgive them. Then there are the personality types who talk about forgiveness, yet deep down inside suppress their true feelings. They house anger and resentment in the name of forgiveness. Finally, there are the personality types who will always take full responsibility for everything that happens. These are the people who believe that it is always their fault. They take the position that forgiving others is not applicable. For these people, forgiveness of self becomes important.

I find that there is a lot of confusion around what forgiveness really means. Consequently, people have a hard time integrating it into their lives. First, forgiveness does not mean that you must forget what happened to you. Second, it does not mean that it is all right for another person to take advantage of you or to violate you. Forgiveness simply means to *stop feeling resentment*. It means releasing any negatively charged emotional energy that you are holding with respect to a situation, an event, or a person. When you practice forgiveness, you free up your divine energy to do its work. You let go of the energy that has a negative hold on you, that is sucking the life out of you. You call in energy that allows you to heal. You add vital healthy energy back into your energy system, and you put life back into your body.

Emotions Tell the Story

If you look at your spirit as your connection to life itself, and your emotions as your interpreter, then your emotions will tell you how you are living your life. They will always reveal your true feelings. They will tell you by their energetic charge if they are strengthening your connection to life or weakening it by drawing both life and energy out of you. If you hold on to old emotional hurts, fears, and life's traumas, then you use up enormous amounts of energy trying to sustain something that in reality is disconnecting you from your life. Holding on to any emotion that does not serve you well makes no sense at all because it will rob you of everything: quality of life, energy, good health, enjoyment, love, happiness, joy, peace, meaningful relationships, and abundance—all of the things that both God and our spiritual selves believe we are worthy of having in this lifetime.

The Mental Layer of Energy

It is through the mental layer of energy that I get my first real sense of how a person relates to and interacts with their external world. This layer of energy, just like the spiritual and emotional layers, is multifaceted. The information contained within this layer provides insight into a person's biological "weak sites"; the genetic coding that identifies their personality traits; how they mentally function; and their perceptions, beliefs, attitudes, and values. It also reveals whether they flow with predominantly masculine or feminine energy.

It is our genetic coding that identifies our primary brain determinants, meaning how we mentally process information. What I am referring to is, does the person have a greater preference for left-hemisphere functioning or right-hemisphere functioning when it comes to their decision-making process? While it is not entirely accurate to say that a person is either/or, since both hemispheres actually work together all of the time, there does tend to be a genetic predisposition for one over the other. That predisposition appears to be determined by the genetic coding of their personality traits. The personality is what defines core preferences of mental functioning. For example, people who have a left-hemisphere predisposition tend to see their external world as linear and well defined, black and white. These people tend to use five senses in their mental processing (sight, hearing, touch, taste, or smell). People who have right-hemisphere predisposition tend to see their external world as open and unstructured and prefer neither black nor white. They are comfortable dealing in the gray areas. They are multisensory, meaning that they instinctively integrate their sixth sense (intuition) into their mental processing. While in reality we each have the capacity to mentally multitask, meaning that we can fully utilize both hemispheres effectively when gathering information, we tend to stay within our core personality traits when it comes to making decisions.

Once I get a clear understanding of a person's mental functioning, then I can move forward to determine their personality type. By doing so, I will know where in the physical body to look for their biological weak sites, the specific areas within the body that are most susceptible to energetic imbalance and illness. Each of us has a weak site, and interestingly enough, that weak site is identified by our brain determinants and by the genetic coding of our personality traits. I will be discussing in detail the role personality plays in our lives in Part III of this book. However, I would like to add at this time that as science has delved deeper into the study of personality and brain functioning, it is becoming more clear that the two are inseparable.

Perceptions, Attitudes, Values, and Beliefs

The mental layer is also where I get a sense of a person's perceptions, attitudes, and values. Those include the things that they strongly believe in and hang on to because they know them to be true. They willingly accept them as true because their conscious mind can readily attach a current-life experience or emotion to them. Let's first begin by examining how perceptions shape our lives.

Perceptions influence whether we attach negative or positive emotional energy to our life experiences. They make up the framework we use for establishing our attitudes and values. Each of us starts accumulating perceptions very early in life because as children we are always being told what to think, how to behave, what is right and wrong, and what we should believe in. As we grow older, we often experience confusion, conflict, and energetic imbalance within our mental layer because our old perceptions do not fit with our current life experiences. We forget to take the time to sort out old perceptions and get rid of the ones that no longer make sense. Once they cease to fit our life, perceptions clutter our thoughts, color our emotional reactions, and distort our beliefs.

If and when we finally do take the necessary steps to let go of old perceptions, then we can at the same time discard attitudes around those perceptions. Attitudes are how we feel about something: a person, a group of people (prejudices), an object, or an idea. If we feel strongly about something, we place value on it. When we do that, we make it a part of our value system. We immediately take on an ownership attitude and decide that no one is going to take it away from us. We hang on to our values as tightly as we can, vowing never to let them go. They become the foundation by which we formulate our belief system. They are important because they affect the decisions we make in life, and they influence our behavior.

If at any time our lives demand that we change and we are challenged to let go of our values, we automatically experience fear and inner conflict. We are afraid deep down inside to let go of values because they represent to the outside world who we are and what we believe in. They set the guidelines and boundaries by which we live our lives, and we hang on to them as if they were our identification badges. We believe that values are what set us apart from everyone else. It is only natural for us to resist any change that requires us to alter our value system or let go of what we believe in. However, the harder we resist letting go of values that no longer fit in our lives, the more inner conflict we experience and the more obvious it becomes that we must let go. Our fear is that if we let go of our old values and have not reestablished new ones, then how are we to live our lives?

Changing our perceptions and attitudes is a lot easier than trying to change our value system. Taking on this challenge requires significantly more energy, more mental and emotional effort, and much more inner trust. The primary reason that we so strongly resist letting go of values is that they influence how we feel about ourselves. The analogy I use for describing values is that they are like comfortable old shoes. When you put them on, they feel good. However, at some point, they are no longer usable. When this happens, you will have to make the decision whether to keep them, even though you cannot wear them, or throw them away. If you hang on to them, they become clutter. I have worked with many people who have mental closets full of clutter with respect to old perceptions, attitudes, values, and beliefs. After a time, there is no more room in their closets. Things that just sit around and take up space also collect tremendous amounts of dust.

Have you checked your mental closet lately? I would like to offer the suggestion that you evaluate your life and run your own diagnostic checkup to determine if you are holding on to things that do not fit anymore. If so, then perhaps it is time to get rid of them.

The Two Forces of Energy

The final area in which I seek understanding before moving on to the physical layer has to do with a person's duality of energy flow. Each one of us has two different energy forces that flow throughout both our energy body and our physical body. These two energy forces, while cellularly programmed to work cooperatively, actually oppose each other in their energetic polarity. One energy force has a positive charge to it and flows masculine energy. The other energy force has a negative charge to it and flows feminine energy. The catalyst that regulates the interaction between these two energy forces is the endocrine system and the secretion of its hormones. Each chakra, the associated organs, and each one of the seven endocrine glands responds chemically to either positive or negative electrical charges. The one gland, one organ, and four chakras that are neutral in polarity—meaning they are both masculine and feminine in their charge—are the pineal gland (7th chakra); the heart (4th and 11th chakras); and the divine source (13th chakra).

As with your other biological genetic coding, such as your personality traits and mental functioning, you also have cellular genetic coding that responds chemically to your preference of one energy flow over the other. For example, if a person's genetic coding for their mental functioning and personality type dictates that decision making is left-hemisphere oriented, then that person will flow masculine energy as their predominant force. If, however, decision making is mainly right-hemisphere oriented, then that person will flow feminine energy as their predominant force.

When you think of masculine and feminine energy, do not think of these concepts in terms of male or female gender. Think of them as qualities that reside within both sexes. In fact, it is actually easier to understand the difference between the two if you were to associate their energy with behavior. Each energy force has its own specific function, its own behavioral pattern, its own special skills, and its own uniqueness. Masculine energy communicates how you function mentally and physically, meaning your external orientation to life. It drives you to approach life from the physical to the spiritual (external to internal). Feminine energy communicates how you function emotionally and spiritually, meaning your internal orientation toward self. Feminine energy reverses the approach and encourages you to come from the spiritual to the physical (internal to external).

Masculine energy acts as the catalyst that allows you to synthesize your feminine, spiritual, intuitive insights into words and thoughts so they can be applied to your external world. Feminine energy provides a more holistic approach to life so you can see it from a variety of perspectives. Think of your feminine energy as your peripheral vision. It expands your viewpoint and opens up the awareness of your conscious mind, allowing you to see the whole picture. Your masculine energy is a more closely focused perspective, which wants you to only see what is directly in front of you. To help you better understand the difference between the two energy forces, let's look at their differences, as associated with behavioral characteristics.

Masculine Energy

Masculine energy focuses more on activity than receptivity. It drives you to participate in life, to be a doer. Its motivation is externally driven. Masculine energy primarily utilizes left-hemisphere thinking; therefore, it is analytical in nature and relies on logic. It depends explicitly on the five senses for information processing. It takes all incoming information and processes it sequentially, then makes decisions based on facts and historical precedent rather than emotions. It is detail oriented and is aggressive when it needs to be. It is independent and views life as a competitive event. It measures success based on results, not on effort.

Masculine energy demands that you conquer your fears. It wants you to approach them as if they were competitors where there will be only one winner. It wants you to participate in life from the perspective that says take what you need—disregarding everyone else. It sees life as a solo performance and you are the only performer. It demands that you are always in control: control over your emotions, your environment, and the people in your life. Masculine energy drives the need for closure. It is reluctant to change. It would rather have you stay with what is familiar: old patterns of behavior, old perceptions, old attitudes, and old values, rather than having to exert the energy to create new ones. The old and familiar it understands. Masculine energy fuels the human ego. It provides the fortitude and determination needed to survive. It communicates directly with the physical body, telling it to give you the energy needed to help you cope with your life challenges in a straightforward fashion. It is more concerned with personal safety, physical needs, status, power, and wealth. Masculine energy's wisdom reveals itself through the material world and the accumulation of possessions. It measures health solely on how effectively the body and mind communicate. It does not take spirit into consideration.

Feminine Energy

Feminine energy is the inner voice in the back of your mind. It tells you when you must change the parts of your life that are fostering dependency and are setting you up for emotional hurt. It encourages you to investigate the unknown and sees change as a new beginning. It is your inner knowing that reveals itself through introspection. Its motivation is internally driven, and it sees life as a cooperative effort that promotes collaboration and encourages partnerships. It thrives on relationships with others and demands that you trust your instincts and intuitive insights. It seeks environments that are supportive and nurturing and nudges you to learn to dance with your fears, to befriend them and learn from them. When they become your friends, then they lose their negative hold on you.

Feminine energy's gentle persistence pushes you to let go of old patterns of behavior, old perceptions, old attitudes, and old values that no longer serve you well. Though always gentle in nature, it will continually encourage you to move forward. Abhorring stagnation, it is relentless in its effort to remind you that fears take away your personal power. It comforts you when you need it, and it embraces you with its energy in a loving way that allows your fears to subside naturally and gradually and eventually be replaced by positive lessons and feelings. It wants you to be open and receptive—not closed and unyielding. Its energy embodies the essence of your spirit, and its strength carries you through times of real need. Feminine energy believes that all is one, and it aligns you with the circle-of-life philosophy: *Take what you need but replace what you take*. It reminds you to laugh and it nags you to play. Its approach to life is through simplicity, not complexity, and it is passive yet persistent in encouraging you to move forward and let go of the past. It focuses more on right-hemisphere functioning; therefore, it incorporates the use of intuition in the processing of information and feeling in decision making. It reminds you to "just be," since it is more interested in the quality of life than material possessions. Feminine energy reveals its wisdom through the stories of your life. It measures health through the totality of who you are and how effectively all aspects of you are communicating—meaning body, mind, and spirit.

Balancing Masculine and Feminine Energy

For approximately the last 5,000 years, civilizations have embraced masculine energy as the dominant energy. During these times, societal beliefs have virtually repressed feminine energy by disregarding its contribution. Those who flowed feminine energy throughout these millennia have always struggled, trying to fit into a world that placed no real value on the qualities of nurturing and care giving, intuition, or being emotional. For all this time, most believed that the only place for these qualities was in the home—never in the world of business or politics. Only recently have these old perceptions and attitudes begun to change. New values and beliefs are emerging. As we move forward from the Piscean Age into the Aquarian Age, the development of feminine energy will continue to be encouraged and embraced as a much-needed balancing force. The primary reason is that the Aquarian Age is feminine in its electrical charge. Those who flow masculine energy will struggle with the changes taking place in the 21st century. However, unlike the other ages, the Aquarian Age is not about suppressing or devaluing either energy. It is about creating a compatible balance between the two. The rallying cry for the Aquarian Age will be balance, alchemy, and expansion. This era will be about the balancing of one's own internal energy forces so that transformation of consciousness can be expanded.

Even though our genetic coding determines if we flow predominantly one energy over the other, it is important to remember that we all have both energy forces flowing within us. It is possible to create balance between masculine and feminine energy—to create a "sacred marriage" of sorts; and to create an energetic, neurological, and chemical alliance between spirit, mind, and body. This is an alliance that will allow us to individually access and fully utilize our God-given talents in such a way that we can turn potential into reality. In fact, the balancing of one's energy forces will be crucial if we are to evolve as a species.

Balance is attainable if we learn how to integrate the unique qualities that each of these energy forces offers in our daily lives. Through integration, we maximize the individual strengths of masculine and feminine energy in such a way that neither feels compromised. Our lives will no longer feel like a game of tug-of-war, or a battle between head and heart. When we live life through balance, we create a newly evolved energetic force within ourselves. We become "spiritually androgynous," meaning that spiritually we are neither specifically masculine nor feminine. In this balanced state, we open the portal (7th chakra) through which we can access a deeper, more intimate relationship with ourselves. We can enjoy living life from the energy of the divine (13th chakra), and we can tap into an energetic force charged with strong healing energy (10th chakra). The key to finding balance and unlocking the portal through which you can access your higher self lies within the spiritual sacred energy found in your heart (4th and 11th chakras), which flows both masculine and feminine energy. It is the fulcrum point between your spiritual world and your physical world.

Life lived without balance will mean living with the constant battle between the conscious and subconscious minds. The battle between the minds inhibits the ability to create the life and health we so desire. It keeps us locked into old patterns of behavior that prevent us from moving forward in our personal development and spiritual growth. The confusion generated by the battle of the conscious and subconscious minds creates a chemical imbalance within the body that makes it more susceptible to illness. Those illnesses tend to surface first within our weak sites. Chemical imbalances between the body and mind create a frenzied, chaotic energy that interpenetrates all layers of the energy system. This chaos drains us energetically. It creates mental, emotional, and physical stress and weakens our immune system. It prevents the body from healing the way it is designed to.

The Physical Layer of Energy

Proceeding with the session, I now consolidate all of the information I have intuitively gathered and combine it with what my sight actually shows me. What I am reading at this point is the physical body and the physical layer of energy. This validates what my intuitive impressions have already brought forth. By watching the dynamics of the person's energy system, I am able to put the pieces of the puzzle together and do it in such a way that it will be of value to the person. However, by the time I get to this point, I already have a good idea of where I will find the root cause of any illness and what created it.

The physical body, as well as the physical layer of energy, reveals how we actually interface with the outside world. The information contained within this energy layer is a current, up-to-date reflection of what is happening in the present moment. It exhibits how we communicate verbally, our learning modalities, and our personality characteristics. It does this by creating specific language patterns, habits, and emotional and psychological patterns of behavior. The physical layer of energy is the most complex of all the layers. This psychophysical structure carries within it all of the information contained throughout our other energy layers, as well as our biological genetic coding, which will determine many facets of who we are physically.

The physical layer of energy acts as our sentinel. It watches over everything we do and warns us of any situation that may jeopardize our personal safety or our security. It communicates its findings by setting off warning signals within the physical body and relies on the five senses for information and guidance. It depends on our perceptions, attitudes, and values to guide its behavior. It is always in direct communication with our mental layer of energy. Ego drives much of the behavior we display from this layer of energy. The physical layer of energy is where we store information around societal and family beliefs; along with the mental layer, it is where we store learned information. It relies on past experience as its primary means of making decisions. When we approach life only from a physical perspective, there is a tendency to create perceptions that contain inadequate information. Without integrating emotions or intuition into the decision-making matrix, the choices we make in life can be flawed and will not be in our overall best interest.

The physical body is the dumping site for all energetic imbalances. Any imbalances, whether mild or severe, will eventually surface here. For example, if your energy system is healthy and all layers are energetically balanced, then your physical body will feel strong and vital. You will experience a high level of energy. On the other hand, if your energy system is depleted or in disarray, then your physical body becomes tired, weak, and susceptible to the formation of illness.

Reading the Physical Energy Layer

During a session, I first look at the overall health of the energy field. I look to see if its energy force is flowing freely from the top of the head to the bottom of the toes. I look for protrusions (energy buildup), congestion (restricted flow), or depletion (loss of energy). I check out each chakra to see if it is open or closed—that is, whether it is energetically active or dormant. Next, I move into the body itself, starting at the head. I determine if there are any chemical imbalances within the brain itself. I look at each endocrine gland to get a feel for its functioning. I look at the person's weak site to see if there are any imbalances or malfunctions. I then look to see what other areas of the body are being affected. If other areas *are* affected, then I check on the severity. I look for abnormalities in cellular structure, degeneration of skeletal structure, muscle rigidity and toxicity, tumors, congenital disorders, and major system dysfunctions.

When I come across an area that is vibrationally out of balance or where I see anything out of the ordinary for that particular person, I spend time there and make note of the colors. The colors within the person's energy field will tell me if the malfunction originated within the spiritual, emotional, mental, or physical layers. I determine if there is immune system involvement, and if so, how much. This helps me understand the severity of the malfunction and tell whether it originated externally; that is, whether it is some sort of viral infection. If I find any area of the body where there are signs of distress, imbalance, or malfunction, I will stay with that area until I get a clear reading on what is happening. For example, if I am scanning a person's body and I find that the liver has to work extra hard to perform its normal functions, then the energy in that area will be protruded. If the color red is present in this area, then I look for inflammation. If I see the color of dark red/brown, then I know that there is central nervous system involvement. This color indicates a general buildup of toxins within the body and particularly the liver. Once I determine the status of the liver, then I check out the lungs and heart to see if either of these areas are part of the cause.

Next, I move to the pancreas and intestinal tract to determine if the person's digestive system is working properly. Is there proper assimilation and elimination? If not, I want to know why and what change would have caused the malfunction. Did the person change their diet? Have they overindulged in sweets? If I find that there is a blood sugar imbalance, I will check the pancreas. Then I will check out the thyroid gland to get a feel for the person's metabolism. When I read the body, it is just like trying to solve a mystery. I keep looking for clues to help me link the pieces together.

The Origin of Illness—Two Different Perspectives

I will end this chapter by addressing the origination of illness. One of the primary beliefs that separates physicians from alternative practitioners is that physicians believe that all illness originates *externally*, while alternative practitioners believe that all illness originates *internally*. I believe that both are correct. While I generally approach my work from the perspective that all illness originates internally within the energy system, I have read many people where this was not the case. There are environmental contaminants that are so toxic to the body that when a person is exposed to them for a prolonged period of time, they overwhelm all systems and prevent them from functioning properly. When this is the case, then both the physical body and energy system struggle to maintain balance. Without balance we become ill.

Tom—Age 32

To help illustrate my point, I would like to share the session with Tom, who at age 31 was diagnosed with Amyotrophic Lateral Sclerosis (ALS, or Lou Gehrig's Disease). When I asked Tom why he came to see me, he said he hoped that I would tell him the doctors were wrong in their diagnosis. I told him they were not. His energy system and the colors contained within it confirmed the doctors' findings. However, what I did not see in his energy field were the normal colors or patterns of energy that would indicate that the illness originated because of some strong emotional, mental, or spiritual imbalance. My first instinct was that perhaps what I was seeing was somehow not accurate. What caused my skepticism was that other clients with ALS whom I had read clearly showed signs that their illness originated within one of the internal energetic layers. I started asking questions to help get a better feel for his energy, but nothing came up that was a positive indicator that Tom's illness indeed had an energetic origin.

Other than normal childhood diseases, Tom had been a very healthy, vital young man. He was not aware of any family genetic history for this type of illness, so it seemed illogical to him that ALS was what he had. While his illness was just in the beginning stages, it appeared to be progressing rapidly throughout his body. Tom's energy field did not show any signs of emotional or psychological trauma that would weaken it enough to cause a predisposition for this type of illness. For the most part, he ate right, honored his biological needs, exercised, did not smoke, did not drink caffeine or colas, and did not drink alcoholic beverages. He meditated daily and loved the outdoors. He had a healthy connection with the divine and honored his spiritual essence. He had a strong will to live, and his energy reflected a positive outlook on life. He seemed to be doing what health-care practitioners would say is right. With this being the case, he wanted to know why he would get something as severe and irreversible as ALS.

When I went into his physical body, it immediately became very clear that the cause of the illness was created externally by some kind of environmental contamination. First, I saw a breakdown of communication within his immune system. The colors indicated that it was severely overworked and compromised. I then observed that his lungs were damaged. Tom's breathing was shallow, and he had difficulty fully expanding his lungs. His body showed signs of oxygen deprivation. As I continued to move throughout his body, I kept seeing signs that something had violated and weakened his body in a way that made him vulnerable to this illness. I continually got intuitive impressions around his being exposed to environmental toxins. It appeared that the exposure was enough to impact his bodily functions.

I asked Tom if he had been exposed to toxic substances, high levels of heavy metals, or fertilizers. He answered yes, that was part of his job. I told him that I could not really attach the root cause of his illness to any imbalances within the spiritual, emotional, or mental layers of energy. I believed the cause was external; the exposure he had been subjected to affected his immune system. I asked him if he had been sick prior to being diagnosed. He said about eight months before, he'd started noticing muscle weakness and cramping within his left arm and left leg; he had been quite ill. The doctors were unable to determine what his ailment was; however, they too thought it may have something to do with his line of work. They suggested bed rest so his body could fully recover.

He never really did regain his strength and was eventually diagnosed with ALS. I did see some slight emotional undertones that certainly contributed to his susceptibility; however, I agree with the physicians that the real cause was external. The reason I determined that there was some emotional energy attached to the situation is because Tom thought that his illness forced him to get out of a profession that he was afraid would eventually would kill him.

People think me strange when I say that illness is a wonderful teacher. However, I believe it to be true. When we become ill, we are forced to slow down, to reevaluate our priorities, to rebalance our lives, and to work at realigning ourselves with our divine and the natural healer each of us has within. Illness is not just time off work. It is an opportunity to learn. Tom chose to see his illness as an opportunity to take charge of his own healing and learn from the experience. He now uses a computer as his only communication link with others. He wears special headgear with a mouse on top and a tube that he blows air into to move the cursor on the screen. He is going to start his own support group via the Internet and plans to bring hope to others with ALS by sharing what he himself has learned. Tom is truly turning lemons into lemonade.

Life—an Endless Cycle of Lessons

Over the course of my 17 years as a medical intuitive, I have come to realize that life is truly a mystical experience. It is an endless cycle of lessons cleverly disguised to act as catalysts to readjust our thinking. Each and every experience forces us to look at our inner self and how we are living our lives; each opens up our awareness. The lessons we learn from our experiences provide insight and wisdom when we need it. Our lessons become the stories of our lives, the reflection of whom we will be tomorrow. They act as navigators plotting our life paths, and assist us in making the choices that will determine whether we fulfill our sacred contracts. We take our lessons with us every step of the way and use them as reminders that we must stay on course. If we were to look at our life experiences as opportunities to learn instead of just something that happens, we would value life differently. We would see that each lesson provides a tremendous opportunity for us to better understand ourselves and others. Each lesson and its wisdom would bring us closer to understanding our own truth, putting us in touch with our true essence. Our lives would take on new meaning.

Remember that life gives you what you ask for. Through your lessons, you transform yourself into a powerful magnet attracting back to yourself whatever you send out. Your energy system is responsible for translating those lessons energetically and determining where the lessons will be stored cellularly within your physical body. The light of your energy system reflects how your lessons are affecting you. Your emotions reveal how you really feel about them. Your personality expresses to the external world what you have learned through your lessons. And, your physical body lives those lessons.

I hope that through my explanations and stories, you can better understand the valuable information contained within the human energy system. Most importantly, I hope that you can begin to see that all of life's lessons lead you to the understanding that you are on a journey—one that holds within it the mysteries that reveal your true self. I have been shown over and over again through readings that if you look at your life through the eyes of your spiritual self, then life becomes an exciting voyage of wonderment and self-discovery.

🦋

Reflection
The mightiest redwood in the grove consists of
a series of individual layers, one atop the other.
We, too, consist of a series of layers. They are the spiritual, emotional,
mental, masculine, feminine, and physical energy layers.
Those layers are constantly interacting within us,
affecting us every moment of our lives.
Good health is the result of maintaining
each of those layers at peak performance.

🦋 🦋 🦋

6

The Human Energy System
As a Diagnostic Tool

*"Intuition is the sensory system which operates
without data from the five senses."*
— Gary Zukav, author of *The Seat of the Soul*

Throughout history, there is evidence that medical intuition has been used for diagnosis. The first recorded writings of such skills were by the Pythagoreans in 500 B.C. They held that there was a luminous body of light around a person that could produce a variety of effects in the human body, including the causing and the curing of illnesses. These ancient Greeks were known for their uncanny knack for intuiting the nature of things. It was also in 500 B.C. that Hippocrates first proposed a comprehensive mind and body theory linking health, illness, and personality. In the 14th century, it was Paracelsus, an alchemist and physician, who used intuition and his ability to read energy as part of his diagnostic process. He called the energy he saw *Illistar*, and the information contained within this energy revealed where in the body illness was occurring.

In the 1800s, Franz Anton Mesmer introduced the technique that came to be known as mesmerism. Mesmer discovered that patients who entered a trance state were able to use their intuition to access a different level and quality of information. It is his work that eventually became the foundation for psychiatry and psychology. It was not, however, until the 19th century that the first formal study of intuitive diagnosis occurred using mesmerism as the foundation. The study was conducted by Dr. John Elliotson, a British physician who used the technique of mesmerizing to entrance and anesthetize his subjects. While in this state, he found that they could use their intuition to access information for the purpose of identifying illnesses. Elliotson would take his mesmerized subjects to hospitals and ask them to use their intuition to identify illnesses that were baffling physicians. The accuracy with which they could diagnose illness was both uncanny and astonishing. Needless to say, when Elliotson reported his findings to his conservative colleagues in the medical profession, they were not openly embraced. His innovative ideas and his approach did not fit within the parameters of traditional medicine.

In 1911, Dr. William Kilner, a medical doctor, reported his findings on the use of intuition as a means of exploring the human energy system. Kilner found that the "aura" differed considerably from patient to patient depending on sex, mental ability, and health. His studies showed there was a direct connection between illness and what he would see in the energy system. He found that certain diseases showed up as patches or irregularities of energy within the energy field. He used this information to diagnose a variety of ailments, such as liver dysfunction, tumors, epilepsy, and psychological disturbances.

It was also in this century that the most widely known medical intuitive diagnostician lived. Edgar Cayce (1877–1945), who was known as "The Sleeping Prophet," used his intuitive insight for the purpose of medical diagnoses. While Cayce was able to read many aspects of a person intuitively, his focus was centered on the health of the energy body and the physical body. Cayce gave extensive readings on the effects of attitudes and emotions on one's health. He emphasized that negatively charged emotions released toxins from the glandular system of the body. He stated that these toxins would create imbalances that would deplete one's energy. They would block the elimination process and generally make a person more susceptible to the creation of disease. Cayce also professed that anger created stomach problems and headaches, that depression weakened the immune system, and that fear was the root cause of heart problems.

In his writings, he discussed the interrelationship between stress and disease. He discussed the human energy system and its holographic imaging of the physical body.

Cayce considered each "entity" (what he called a person) to have three aspects of energy—physical, mental, and spiritual. He believed the mind and body to be vehicles through which the spirit could express itself externally. Cayce suggested that all illnesses are the result of overloads and blockages in these three aspects of energy. In one of his readings, Cayce said, "Healing of the physical without change in the mental and spiritual aspects brings little real help to the individuals in the end." It is Edgar Cayce's work and the information gathered through his readings that has laid the groundwork for contemporary intuitive diagnosticians to follow. His work resulted in some of the most comprehensive studies ever done on the connection between health and spirituality.

Since Edgar Cayce's time, there have been many other gifted healers and intuitive diagnosticians who have come forward to share their unique skills. Each has brought forth their own individual means of expressing how they use their intuition for diagnostic purposes. Some of these people include Dr. Edward Bach, Olga Worrall, Louise L. Hay, Dr. Robert Leitchman, Dr. John Pierrakos, Barbara Ann Brennan, Mona Lisa Schulz, and Dr. Caroline Myss. I am sure that there are many others who are very skilled in intuitive diagnoses who are quietly doing their work to help people understand the relationship between the human energy system and illness. If you are one of them, I encourage you to come forward. The need is greater than the supply.

A Diagnostic Tool for Reading the Physical Body

As a diagnostic tool, the human energy system acts as an imaging and monitoring system that reflects all changes occurring within the energy body and the physical body. When there is illness (imbalance) in the energy body, it communicates this information by creating blockages, protrusions, congestion, or depletion within the energy field. Any time these energetic factors occur, there is potential for the physical body to become susceptible to infection or disease. The human energy system is designed to act as an early detection system alerting the brain and the cells of the body that something is out of sync. When the brain receives a message from the human energy system that imbalance is occurring, it sends out electrical impulses to the specific site within the body where there is imbalance. The depth of information that the human energy system can provide to the brain is very substantial. It can provide feedback to pinpoint the origin of the imbalance. It can also provide feedback on the condition created by the imbalance and its severity. Since the energy body and the physical body mirror each other, the energy system will instantly reflect what is changing and how that change is affecting the physical body.

When the energy body becomes ill, there are two distinct ways in which that illness will surface in the physical body. The first is that there will be an overall feeling of energy loss. The energy field will actually reduce its size in order to protect the healthy energy it has left. The physical body reacts by becoming tired. Second, the energy system tells the brain to send messages via the endocrine system, alerting the physical body that something is out of balance. The endocrine system communicates the imbalance by secreting a variety of chemicals that affect both the nervous system and the immune system. The physical body reacts by creating either a mild or extreme stress reaction. The physical results are an adrenaline rush, increased heart rate, and a change in breathing patterns. If the imbalance is mild, then the physical body responds in subtle ways, which may include mild headaches, indigestion, or muscle tension. However, if the imbalance is extreme or continues for a prolonged period of time (meaning that it becomes chronic), then the body may progress to the point of complete physical breakdown.

It should be noted that not every change in the energy system ends up manifesting itself into a physical dysfunction. The fact is that we are always changing the body's physiology for the better or worse every second of our lives. Since the energy system is a dynamic force, there are many situations we experience daily that cause it to change and fluctuate. For the most part, many of those changes go unnoticed. The primary factor that determines if any change manifests itself into a physical dysfunction is our emotional reaction to those changes. If our emotional reaction is negative or we are resistant to the change, then the energy system will sound the alert, and the physical body will respond accordingly.

The Willingness to Change

Over the course of reading the human energy system and working with people to help them better understand the relationship between their energy system, their emotions, and their illnesses, an interesting truth has presented itself, which is: while many people say they want to heal, most are not willing to change the emotional and psychological patterns that lead to the creation of their illness. I have found some cases where their illness was even feeding an emotional need. Here is a session that will show you what I mean.

Suzanne—Age 51

Suzanne came to me for a general health checkup. She was having some health issues and wanted to know if there were energy blockages that were preventing her from getting well. The first thing on her list was to have me check on the progression of her diabetes. I found her request interesting because she did not show any of the normal energetic signs of being diabetic. Her blood sugar level was somewhat low but did not indicate any real problem. I asked her if she was seeing a doctor or endocrinologist for her diabetes. She said that she was; however, she was very frustrated because the doctors were not helping her. It seemed that she had changed doctors many times because none of them would diagnose her as diabetic. One doctor did say that there was a predisposition for hypoglycemia but no diabetes. This caused

Suzanne great emotional distress because she knew that she had the illness and had lived with it for the last 25 years. To show you how convinced she was that she had the disease, she even brought food to the session so she could maintain her body's chemical balance.

I told her that I too had to agree with the doctors. Neither her energy system nor her body were showing the signs of diabetes. She got angry and told me that she *did* have it and that we were all totally wrong. Her strong emotional reaction surprised me since I thought she would be relieved to hear the confirmation. I asked her to help me understand why she was so angry and to explain what led her to believe she had this illness. What she shared clearly illustrated the impact our emotions can have on the mind and body.

Suzanne told me that 25 years ago, she went to her family doctor for an annual physical, and he did a blood test. When she returned to get her results, he told her that her sugar level was a little high and that he wanted to monitor the situation to be sure that she was not showing the early signs of diabetes. When he told her this, it totally distressed her. It seems that diabetes was common on her mother's side of the family, and her worst fear loomed right in front of her. She got so upset that by the time she got home she was sick to her stomach. When she told her children what had transpired, they responded in a loving, sensitive way that fed a deep-seated need in her. The more Suzanne dwelled on what the doctor had said, the more emotional energy she attached to it, serving to convince her that she already had the illness.

Now, to help put this all in perspective, 25 years ago there was not as much information on diabetes as there is today. At that time, it was viewed as a serious illness, the symptoms of which were not fully understood. So, the more Suzanne's family discussed the illness, the greater the buildup in her mind. It was finally decided that Suzanne should quit her job for her health reasons and stay home to care for her children. Deep down inside, Suzanne was very pleased by the decision, since that was something that she wanted very much to do; however, she could not because of financial reasons. Already, the illness, even though self-created in a sense, was serving her well. Over the course of the next 25 years, Suzanne held on to this phantom illness as if it were real. She was not about to let go of the belief that she had it because if she did, then she could not stay home as she wanted—and the attention she had become accustomed to receiving might dissipate.

What I found fascinating was that Suzanne's physical body was responding as if she *did* have diabetes. It had become so conditioned and comfortable with the rituals she had set into her daily routine that it was actually going through the motions as if this illness existed.

I suggested to Suzanne that she seek the help of a psychotherapist who could help her work through her emotional issues and work on behavioral modification. Once again she got very angry and proceeded to tell me that if I thought she wanted to get better or even get rid of this illness, I was very mistaken. Why would she want to do that? For 25 years, she had lived with it and it served her well. Her reaction was confusing and troubling to me. I realized that there was nothing more that I could do but to move on to the other questions she had. She had made the choice to sabotage her body and hold on to something that would eventually become a reality. The truth was that she was using her perceived illness as a means of getting attention and manipulating others to take care of her. As long as she held on to this belief and attached so much emotional energy to it, it was not possible for her body to return to any semblance of balance. Not surprisingly, Suzanne called me a year later to tell me that she had just been diagnosed with diabetes. This time the diagnosis was real, and not only did she *have* the disease, but it was in an advanced stage. This was easy to understand, since she had conditioned her body for 25 years to be diabetic. The impact our emotions have on the mind and body connection is truly profound.

Intuition, the Sixth Sense

I am often asked to explain what intuition is. People are curious about what it feels like, and they want to know how it expresses itself. They also want to know when they are using it. And, most important, they want to know how they can develop the trust in it that is necessary to follow its direction. I find that describing intuition is easier than trying to put it into definitive terms, because it expresses itself differently in each person. We are so conditioned to using our five physical senses (sight, hearing, touch, taste, and smell), that we expect intuition to be something equally tangible. We expect it to be black and white, and it is not. Intuition is the sensory process that reveals its information through the pictures it paints in our minds and the quiet inner voice that we hear throughout our body. The five physical senses are easy to understand and relate to. Intuition, the "sixth sense," requires us to *trust*, not to *know*.

Every single one of us is an intuitive being. A person does not have to be psychic to be intuitive or to use their intuition for the purpose of diagnostic analysis of the body. Intuition is one of our natural instincts and is a critical part of our mental processing. In fact, it is so integral that most of the time we take it for granted or are not even aware that we are utilizing it. Intuitive mental processing is usually associated with right-brain functioning. However, it is really whole-brain thinking. We utilize our intuition as a means of providing a different way to look at situations, as a means of getting a well-rounded perspective on what is happening.

Intuition is a like a weather gauge. It tells us what the current conditions are and alerts us when change is in the air. It is the vehicle through which our spirit expresses itself to our external world. It sees the situations and challenges that life throws our way from a holistic point of view. It is the conceptual part of our thinking and is what allows the mind to create ideas. Its spark kindles the flame and fuels the fires that drive us to manifest our dreams. Its energy provides the inspiration needed to encourage us to follow our visions. The use of intuition encourages us to look at possibilities and explore the unknown.

Intuition can often provide the answers to problems when the conscious mind cannot. It does not express itself through the five senses or the left part of our brain, but rather through the pictures, dreams, memories, feelings, and impressions that are stored in the right brain. Intuitive information reveals itself to the conscious mind in the form of emotions, which are then chemically communicated to the physical body through reactions such as hunches, gut feelings, sudden bursts of insight, or flashes of awareness out of the blue. For example, have you ever known someone was going to call even before they do? Or got an idea and just knew that it was a sure-fire winner? Or struggled with a problem only to find the solution in a dream? That was intuition in action.

Another question that people ask me is what can they do to develop or hone their intuitive skills. The first and most obvious answer is to create an awareness around it. Pay attention to how it expresses itself. Then practice integrating it into your daily life so that you will become comfortable with it. The more you use it, the more you will trust it, as well as the information it provides. Another important element in the development of your intuitive skills is not to work hard at being intuitive. Intuition is not something that can be accessed when your mind is active or outwardly focused. It requires a relaxed mind and a relaxed body. Your focus must be internal and introspective. The information it can provide must be allowed to flow freely. It requires time and lack of expectations so it can look at the situation or problem from all perspectives.

The integration of intuition into your daily life heightens your sensory awareness. It empowers you, and it expands your consciousness. It opens up a whole new way of looking at life and prepares you to cope with change. It reduces the amount of anxiety and fear in your life. They are two of our most powerful emotions and capable of creating stress in the physical body and imbalance in the energy body. They are precursors to the creation of illness.

Become Your Own Diagnostician

The energy system is very effective in communicating its state of health. With a little practice, you can perform your own diagnostic checkup. How? The fastest way is by learning to let your hands read your energy field. The hands, and particularly the fingertips, are very sensitive instruments that can scan the physical body to feel where imbalances are occurring. If the energy system is strong and vital, then you will feel an overall warmth over the areas being examined. However, if there is congestion or energy depletion, then you will feel cold spots or there will be areas where you can barely feel any heat at all. If there is chemical overstimulation of an endocrine gland or an energetic protrusion, then the affected area will feel very warm or hot.

Let me share an example to help you understand how the energy system and the physical body affect each other. Let's say you are in a conversation where you are trying to express your thoughts on a particular topic. The problem is that the person you are talking to cannot seem to understand what you are trying to say or cannot appreciate the importance of the point you're trying to make. The more you try to get your point across, the more frustrated you become. As your frustration increases, so does your stress level. This emotional reaction causes the energy system to sound the alarm and warn the body that the reaction is in fact having a negative impact on the physical body.

Now, let's say your frustration turns to anger. The more angry you become, the greater the severity of chemical imbalance in your body. The physical result is that your throat tightens up. The minute this happens, you begin to have difficulty swallowing—perhaps you cough or choke or your voice breaks. These physical reactions are the energy system's way of trying to tell the body to shut down what is creating the imbalance. If you were to scan the throat area at the time this was happening, you would feel a large hot spot (protrusion) of energy in this area. Then, as the emotional reaction subsided, the energy in this area would return to normal and you would just feel a warmth around the throat.

I believe that each of us can become an intuitive diagnostician to some extent. All that is required is that we evolve our intuition to the point where it allows us to read the energy system for the purpose of gathering information and perceiving any malfunctions in the body. With some practice and patience, any person can hone their intuitive skills in such a way that they can accurately read where energy imbalances are occurring in the body. However, there is one important element that you must adhere to if you are to become an accurate diagnostician, and that is the ability to emotionally detach from the person you are reading—not an easy thing to do, especially if the person you are trying to read is yourself. Yet, without the ability to emotionally detach, you contaminate the quality of the information your intuition provides. You will distort the information so it feels safe, or negate what it is telling you as not being valid.

The best way to start the process of becoming your own diagnostician is to learn how to read your own energy and body. Start by paying attention to how your intuition communicates with you. Does it reveal itself through your instinctive feelings? Perhaps it is a gut feeling or a sudden flash of insight, or maybe even those goose bumps you get when you "just know that you know." Pay attention to the impressions that your intuition sends you. Listen to how it tells you that something is out of sync. When you get those feelings, ask your intuition where in the body you are out of sync and what is causing it. If you pay attention, it will even tell you what is needed in order to restore balance. When you are using your intuition to read your body, it is always important to trust your first impressions. They will tell you precisely what is happening within the body. Do not dismiss any impression even if it is disturbing. The impressions you receive first provide a clear picture of what is really occurring, as they have not yet been distorted by your emotions. If you get the message that something is wrong, then act on that information. Your first impressions will always serve you well, and nine times out of ten, they will be right.

You do not have to literally see the human energy system as I do in order to be an energetic diagnostician. You can develop a skill called symbolic sight. In fact, many gifted healers and intuitive diagnosticians work from symbolic sight. Symbolic sight is where you look for the symbolism of what is happening in your life and connect that symbolism to what is happening within your physical body. For example, when a person feels that life is beating them up, then their body responds by feeling beat up and tired. When craving sweets, then maybe they are craving sweets in other parts of their life such as self-esteem, financial abundance, love, and relationships. Breathing problems symbolize the feeling of being stifled. Being financially strapped shows up in the lower back. Inability to face life shows up through mental illness. Never being good enough manifests as autoimmune diseases and anemia.

Diagnostic Keys

Learn to listen to your emotions. Spend time with them. Do not rush to hide them or make them go away. Emotions provide direction. They are indicators that send very clear messages of how you are feeling both energetically and physically. If you are feeling positive and optimistic, then your energy level increases and your whole body responds by feeling good. If you are feeling depressed, then your energy level decreases; your body becomes tired and lethargic. Confusion causes a chemical imbalance in the brain, and your thinking becomes cloudy. The feeling of being out of control causes an energy loss throughout your entire body. Resentment drains energy from your stomach area. The feeling of being taken advantage of causes a loss of energy in your heart. Anger toward others drains the lower extremities of energy. Your emotions can even tell you if you're holding on to old emotional hurts and if you are using those hurts to manipulate others to get what you want or to feel sorry for you.

Begin to pay attention to how you interact with the people in your life: family, friends, and co-workers. Do you surround yourself with people who energize you or drain you? How do you react emotionally to these types of people? Do the people in your life support you, or do they want you to be dependent on them? Do they enable you to stay emotionally wounded, or do they encourage growth and change? Always listen to your intuition when it comes to dealing with others. It will provide a clear picture of what is really happening. Learn to read your behavioral patterns when around others. If your behavior is submissive, then you will attract people who will try to control you. If you send out the message that you are emotionally vulnerable, then people will sense that and take advantage of you. Is your behavior telling people you are a victim? If so, that might help explain why you keep attracting individuals who are domineering and aggressive.

Take a daily pulse check of your energy body by doing a body scan. The body-scanning process allows your intuition to participate in your energetic evaluation. It also hones your skill to become sensitive to energetic imbalances. Through the scanning process, you will receive impressions that can tell you where you are both energetically and physically. I find that my morning meditation is the best time for me. Start at your head or crown and work your way down all the way to your toes. Spend time in each section of the body. Run your hands over each part to locate any energy protrusion or depletion. The body is very effective in communicating where there are any imbalances. It will usually convey these imbalances physically through our aches and pains, and areas where we feel discomfort. If a blockage is occurring, then there will usually be some kind of inflammation or heat buildup in that particular part of your body.

The technique of body scanning also fully utilizes your intuitive awareness by bringing attention to the impressions it sends. When you get an impression that alerts you that there is something out of balance, spend time with that impression. Determine where in the body you are sensing it. For example, if you are scanning the body intuitively and get an impression that your stomach is on fire, spend time exploring why it is occurring in this area. Ask yourself some questions. Could the imbalance be caused by something you ate? Have you been under a lot of stress lately, and is this where you are carrying your stress issues? Have you been suffering from frequent indigestion for a prolonged period of time? Is the severity of the discomfort enough to cause your mind to become alarmed? If so, then it is probably time to have it checked out by a physician or a holistic practitioner, depending on your belief system. Remember, the body will tell you what it needs; you just have to take the time to listen.

You can also keep an energy journal. This will help track your energy cycles. Each of us has them. Some of us are morning people, while others are night owls. Some people get their day started energetically at three o'clock in the afternoon, while others are ready for a nap. Know when you feel energized and when you are energetically low. Begin paying attention to what or who drains your energy, and if at all possible, stay away from those things or people when you are in a low cycle. Avoid tasks that require large amounts of energy to be expended in your down times. Stay away from having to deal with emotional issues when you are feeling low. It is too draining, and the results will be less than desired. Also, never deal with emotional issues before you go to sleep, or you will wake up the next day energetically drained and physically tired. Try to deal with emotional issues when you are in your high-energy cycle.

When you first start the process of being your own diagnostician, it may take a bit of getting used to. If you give yourself time, it will become second nature to you. You will find the rewards to be many. There is one thing, though, that I must warn you about: once you allow your intuition to become an active part of your life, you will change. But change is what life is about anyway, isn't it?

Reflection

We use our five physical senses—
sight, hearing, touch, taste, and smell—
to the degree that we are able, on a daily basis.
Intuition is our sixth, and least understood,
sense because it has no physical connection.
Learning to use that sixth sense, and to trust it,
can open up a whole new dimension in solving problems
that we face daily, be they in our interactions
with our world or maintaining our wellness.

7

The Role of a Medical Intuitive

"A practitioner realizes that man is born of spirit and not of matter."
— Ernest Holmes

Medical intuitives are what I call "Puzzle Masters." Their role is to read the body both energetically and physically and to link all the pieces of information together in such a way that they can provide a comprehensive analysis of a person's state of health and overall well-being. Through the use of their intuitive skills, they are able to read energy for the purpose of: 1) identifying where energetic imbalances are occurring; 2) determining their origin; 3) clarifying what is triggering the imbalances, for example emotional and/or psychological issues; 4) identifying how these imbalances are affecting the physical body; 5) analyzing all parts of the body that are being affected; and 6) determining what needs to be done to restore energetic and physical balance. Once a medical intuitive has identified all pieces of the puzzle, then it is their role to present the information in a way that the person can use it to create the changes necessary to regain balance. The primary goal of a medical intuitive should be to lead a person into self-knowledge and then describe ways that the person can facilitate their own healing process.

The benefit of working with medical intuitives is that they can provide a more complete picture of what is creating the potential for illness since they work with all aspects of a person: physical, mental, emotional, and spiritual. They are able to offer insight into the deeper struggles in a person's life that are creating blockages and reveal what needs to be changed in order to restore balance to their lives. I believe that a medical intuitive's greatest purpose is to help their clients connect with the issues that are preventing them from having the life and health they desire.

Should you seek the services of a medical intuitive, it is important not to confuse their services with those of a physician. Medical intuitives do not make medical diagnoses, nor do they prescribe medications. In fact, even the approach that they each take in working with illness and symptoms is different. Physicians work from outside-in and look at the symptoms of the physical body. They believe that illness is the result of external factors. Medical intuitives work from the inside-out. They are more interested in the spiritual, emotional, and psychological issues that create the predisposition for illness to occur. They believe that illness begins internally and manifests itself externally.

Medical intuitives must always be sensitive to the belief systems of the person they are working with. They must take into consideration religious convictions and beliefs in traditional medicine or alternative practices. While it is not the role of the medical intuitive to recommend one method over another or to override a person's principles, it is their responsibility to encourage the person to seek the most expedient course to accelerate the healing process. Alternative healing methods may be very effective. However, if an illness has caused the physical body to become so distressed that it needs immediate attention, then seeing a physician is always recommended.

Medical Intuition As a Profession

If becoming a medical intuitive by profession is of interest to you, then there are some guidelines to consider. First, there must be an *unconditional* willingness to expand your consciousness. People who are skilled medical intuitives invest extensive amounts of time honing their intuitive skills. They have invested time in their own self-development and self-transformation. Second, training is a must. You should be well versed in the areas of basic human behavior, psychology, anatomy, physiology, illness, and ethics applied to intuitive diagnoses. As this book is being written, to my knowledge there is no formal educational curriculum specifically designed to teach medical intuition that is as comprehensive as that of traditional medicine. There are, however, practitioners who have developed their own processes and are currently teaching and providing certification programs.

Medical Teams of the Future

As we move forward into the 21st century, there appears to be a growing open-mindedness toward health and healing occurring within the medical community—a paradigm that may eventually change the way medicine is practiced by medical teams of the future. Perhaps such teams will consist of a physician, a medical intuitive, and alternative practitioners. In essence, allopathic medicine and alternative medicine will complement each other. This combination can be of great value to the patient. Here's why:

1. Each practitioner brings their own expertise, skills, and training to the diagnostic and healing process. The physician and the alternative practitioner work with the patient to restore balance and health to the physical body, and the medical intuitive assists by providing a more comprehensive assessment of the root cause of illness. I should note here that some medical intuitives focus only on being diagnosticians, while others may also take on the role of healing practitioners.

2. Each practitioner has their own way of gathering the necessary information so they can determine the cause of the illness. The physician works with the standard medical history of the person, and the medical intuitive works with the person's beliefs and their biographical history.

3. The physician works to heal the body, while the medical intuitive and alternative practitioner work to heal both body and spirit.

4. Each practitioner understands the importance of listening to the emotional and psychological issues of the patient. Each knows that these issues contribute to the underlying cause of illness. However, what each does with this information is different.

5. When each practitioner's perspective is part of the evaluation and diagnostic process, then the treatment process can be potentially accelerated because recommended approaches will treat both the cause and the effect.

6. Medicine of the future will require treatment of the *whole* person. It will no longer be able to ignore the spiritual essence of the individual.

Thomas Edison, in his infinite wisdom, stated, "The doctor of the future will give no medicine, but will interest his patients in the care of the human frame, in diet, and in the cause and prevention of disease."

I would certainly agree with him. I know from experience, through the physicians I work with, that the combination of physician, medical intuitive, and alternative practitioner is win-win-win for all involved—especially the patient.

🐾

Reflection
Creating and preserving wellness is both a science and an art.
The options, in choosing how we approach wellness,
include addressing physical, mental, and spiritual care.

🐾 🐾 🐾

PART III

Your Personality, Your Health

8

Personality: It's in Your Genes

"Your personality, then, is the material expression. And
your individuality is the personality of the soul."
— Edgar Cayce

Have you noticed that you find yourself attracted to people who are similar to you? There is something subtle about them that magnetically attracts you to them. You feel comfortable with them, and you can relate to their thinking. They treat others in the same way you treat others, and you tend to make them a part of your social network and support system. These people are easy for you to communicate with, and they energize you when you are in their presence.

What about the people you meet or have to deal with who are opposite from you? You get messages that confirm that there is not good chemistry between you, that there is something about them that makes you want to pull back and protect yourself. They drain your energy. The more time you have to spend with them, the greater your awareness becomes of the magnitude of those differences. You struggle to find a common ground on which you can communicate. These people see the world through different eyes, and you realize that they even approach life from another perspective altogether. While it is true that opposites *do* attract, when it comes to building relationships with people who are opposite, the potential for conflict and misunderstanding is high. There will be difficulty finding a common understanding where one or the other does not feel compromised. In order to make these relationships work, each person must be willing to acknowledge and deal with their differences. Each must be willing to commit both time and energy to the relationship—not an easy task unless each becomes aware of why they act the way they do and why they differ.

What is it about people that makes one different from another? What gives each person their own unique individual behavioral characteristics? Why is it that we want to be around people who are like us and have difficulty dealing with people who are opposite? The answer to these questions is two-fold. The first answer has to do with how we energetically disclose ourselves to others. The second has to do with personality.

Each of us externally transmits our own "fingerprint" pattern of energy that communicates to others who we are. That pattern of energy is our personality. When we meet people who are similar in energy pattern and personality, we are attracted to them. When people who are not similar in energy or personality come into our lives, we may at first be attracted to them, yet we soon recognize their differences. If we can cope with or live with the differences, then we will work at building a relationship. However, if we cannot or choose not to deal with the differences, we will move on and seek others who are like ourselves. So, while opposites do attract, they do not necessarily stay together. Sometimes the differences are too great to overcome or do not justify the energy needed to deal with them.

As discussed in the chapter on the language of energy, it is within the mental layer of energy that our personality first reveals itself. That is because the core part of our personality determines our mental functioning. Every aspect of who we are physically and energetically is governed in some way by our personality. Personality has two aspects: inherited and learned. Inherited we cannot change. Learned we can change.

Personality Traits and Characteristics

Each one of us is born with inherent personality traits, meaning our biological genetic coding, that determine the way our brain develops and how our personality expresses itself. That is our core part. Our personality traits reveal themselves at a very early age and remain constant throughout our entire lives. They direct the way we act, how we think, and they establish our learned personality characteristics. Traits create our involuntary habits that determine the course our lives will take. They decide our preferred way of gathering information and how we draw conclusions from the information we take in.

Personality traits influence the choice of words we use to communicate with others, as well as how we learn. Our personality traits are responsible for our brain functioning and its normal neurobiological and biochemical reactions. They establish the electrochemical dialogue that takes place between the brain, the endocrine system, and the physical body. Personality traits reveal themselves through a predominant color found in the human energy system.

The learned parts of personality are called characteristics. Characteristics are the behavioral patterns that we develop as a result of what we have learned. They reflect our biographical history, and they are what makes us unique. They are the distinguishing qualities that differentiate us from others, and they establish our identity and how we express that identity to the outside world. Characteristics are responsible for the formation of habits, comfort zones, quirks, and idiosyncratic behavioral patterns. In the human energy system, our personality characteristics are reflected within the emotional layer of energy. They provide the biographical information that reveals itself through our emotional reactions.

When you combine personality traits and characteristics, you define personality type, meaning the consistent predictable patterns that drive the way we live and why we act the way we do. Personality type represents the orderly arrangement through which we form our perceptions, attitudes, beliefs, and values. Using the premise of

personality type as a categorical formula makes it easier to understand and identify why people are different.

Think of your personality type as your automatic pilot. It creates
the involuntary behavioral patterns necessary for you to function and
survive. Its inherent traits create your own personal road map, which
guides the outward direction you take in life. Its characteristics influence what you become. It affects your self-image, self-esteem, self-
confidence, and self-worth. It motivates you, creates your irritations,
and controls stress and how that stress affects you. Personality
impacts the way you face life's challenges and the coping mechanisms you develop. It is the organizing principle that affects your
sense of reality and spirituality. It greatly impacts your health and
overall sense of well-being.

The History of Personality Type

For centuries, psychologists, psychiatrists, and physicians have
studied personality. They have provided conclusive evidence that
human beings do have distinct personality traits and characteristics
that make them different from one another, and that personality
affects both mental health and physical health. The first person to
classify personality by type was Hippocrates, the father of Western
medicine. He proposed that there were four distinct personality types.
His theory was that a person's personality type determines their vulnerability to mental dysfunction and their susceptibility to illness.
Ever since he declared his findings, there have been many others who
have formed their own theories around personality and illness.

In the 19th century, psychoanalyst Sigmund Freud developed his
own detailed theory of personality. His underlying assumption was
that the body is the sole source of mental energy. He approached personality only from the mental perspective. Soon after Freud's theory
was made public, psychiatrist Carl Jung proposed his own comprehensive theory to explain how personality type affects every aspect of
a person's life. Unlike Freud, Jung integrated the aspect of spirituali-

ty into his theory because of his own beliefs and background. He suggested that behavior was not random, but in fact predictable, and therefore could be classified and observed. Like Hippocrates, Jung postulated that there were four personality types dominated by four distinct modes of psychological functioning: thinking, feeling, sensing, and intuition. While we do have the capacity to use all four of these functions, he theorized, we do not develop them equally.

Jung also believed that people are multisensory in their psychological functioning and do not just rely on the five senses (sight, hearing, touch, taste, smell) for the gathering of information. Jung was of the opinion that the differences in people are the result of inherited core psychological functions associated with how a person gathers information and makes decisions. Through his work, he became aware of core attractions and aversions that people have toward other people, and he noticed that those same attractions and aversions also related to tasks and life events. The more Jung worked with his theory, the better he understood what drives behavior, and the easier it was for him to see personality patterns that make people different.

According to most of the personality theories, we each have within our own personality type both strengths and weaknesses that are primarily determined by the genetic neurological hard-wiring found within our personality traits. The more we function within our inherent core traits (strengths), the stronger and more confident we become, the stronger our sense of reality, the more control we have over our lives, and the better equipped we are to make the choices that create the life and health we want. We are in a stronger position to take advantage of and maximize the opportunities that life sets before us.

If we function outside our core traits and work from our underdeveloped psychological functions (weaknesses), then life loses its synchronicity. We become energetically drained, mentally confused, and experience physical discomfort. Our lives feel like they are out of control, and we have a strong sense of being detached from life. We feel emotionally numb, and our thinking becomes fuzzy. We become mentally immobilized and chemically out of balance. These chemical imbalances create a fight-or-flight stress reaction in the physical body, and that stress response hinders our ability to think clearly even more. As a result, we find ourselves caught up in a vicious cycle of psychological and emotional behavioral patterns that prevent us from getting where we want to go. In the end, we leave ourselves vulnerable to the creation of illness.

The Mind-Body Connection

Edgar Cayce stated, "The spirit is life. Mind is the builder. Physical is the result." Cayce, like many others, believed that what we think is what our body generally becomes. What we have learned is that the mind is the controller of all behavioral and physical functioning and that the power of the mind can intentionally or unintentionally affect both the energy body and the physical body. In other words, we can make ourselves healthy or sick through our thoughts and our emotional reactions to those thoughts. Since those early research studies, more comprehensive studies have taken place to further the understanding of how the mind influences our physical well-being. These studies are validating the premise that there is a direct correlation between personality, thoughts, emotions, and illness.

What has been discovered is that our thoughts and emotions are intertwined, and both play a significant role in the development of disease. If our thoughts are charged with positive energy, then we are emotionally optimistic about life, and we experience an overall sense of well-being. If our thoughts are negatively charged, then we rob the physical body of the energy it needs to maintain balance. Negative thoughts provoke negative emotions: fear, anger, frustration, worry, resentment, and guilt—all of which have an undesirable and potent effect on our ability to fight off disease and infection. Negative thoughts wear down both the energy system and the immune system, leaving a person more susceptible to illness. Those same studies show that prolonged stress also wears down both the energy body and physical body and consequently impacts why people become ill and why they do not heal.

To better understand the mind-body connection, it helps to remember that the human brain is electrical in nature. It communicates its messages to specific sites in the body by sending electrochemical impulses via the central nervous system. These electrochemical impulses and the information they contain activate cellular memory and tell the cellular structure within that specific area of the body how to reorganize itself according to the information being received. If a person is thinking a negative thought, that consequently creates a negative emotional reaction. Then, the brain responds by changing the chemistry in the electrical impulses it sends to the body's systems. These changes in chemistry are what alert the physical body that there is a problem.

Let's say that people's thoughts continually dwell on being sick and tired of their lives. The electrochemical message sent from the brain to the body is that they are sick and tired. If the thought is emotional and is strongly supported, then the body intensifies its reaction by feeling sick and tired. The stronger the thought, the stronger the chemical reaction, and the greater the chances for severe illness to occur. Understanding how the mind electrochemically dialogues with the body makes it is easier to see the direct correlation between state of mind and physical health.

It is important to note that not all thoughts—even those that have a slightly negative undertone—cause illness in the body. If our thoughts are positive and produce positive emotional reactions, then our physical body will continue to function as a healthy, vital unit. It is only the thoughts with strongly negative charges that affect the body and make it susceptible to disease.

To show what I mean, let's use cancer as an example. Psychoneuroimmunology, the study of how emotions affect the immune system, indicates that people who are consumed with negative thoughts or who have a negative outlook on life are more susceptible to the formation of cancer. The same holds true for people who are consumed with negative emotions such as fear, anger, or frustration. Negativity wears down the immune system and leaves the body more susceptible to the creation of disease. On the other hand, people who are optimistic and view life from a positive perspective have stronger immune systems and are able to resist infection and the formation of diseases such as cancer. What has been discovered is that when it comes to good health, positive thoughts play an important role. It also appears that a happy-go-lucky attitude can go a long way in fighting off disease and keeping us healthy.

The Personality and Physical Weak Sites

My own research confirms many of the same findings. It has continually demonstrated that there is a direct connection between personality, the human energy system, chakras, and wellness. It not only substantiates what research has revealed about how a person's mental state influences their susceptibility toward illness, it has also identified that each personality type has its own specific "weak site" within the physical body. Those weak sites are determined by psychological and emotional patterns created by a person's inherent personality traits. In fact, there are relatively specific personality traits that predispose a person to the creation of specific diseases, such as high blood pressure, heart disease, cancer, asthma, tuberculosis, autoimmune disorders, neurological diseases, as well as chronic related illnesses.

By understanding personality type and its associated psychological functioning, we can begin to understand the patterns of behavior that create illness. Through the identification of weak sites, we can determine where the origin of illness will manifest itself in the body. Since I am able to see the energy system and work with the body from the inside out, I have also found that, interestingly enough, a person's personality weak site tends to correspond to their biological weak site. It is within the weak sites that I can identify the origin of illnesses and have a better understanding of how other parts of the body will be affected. The primary difference between the way the energy system and the physical body communicate illness is that the physical body will put up symptoms anywhere in the body, and the energy system pinpoints precisely where the weak site and the root cause of the illness are located.

What I have found is that each personality type's weak site appears to be more sensitive to chemical imbalance than any other part of the body. Part of the reason for this is because of the control that our personality traits have on our psychological functioning and how that functioning affects the brain's biochemistry. In many ways it is our personality that tells the brain how to electrochemically communicate with the body. Taking that premise one step further and connecting the weak sites with specific endocrine glands, organs, and bodily systems, it becomes easier to understand why people become ill in specific areas of the body. It is through our thoughts that we change the chemistry of our body in such a way that it can cause illness to manifest in our weak sites.

My research on personality also stems from the premise that there are four distinct personality types. Each of the four types is determined by their genetic personality coding and how that coding forms their neurological hard-wiring. Each personality type's coding system is what determines their preference toward specific psychological functioning and how that functioning creates the patterns of behavior they exhibit. It is their preferred psychological functioning that delineates the differences in people and the way they gather information and draw conclusions. To help you better understand how personality type affects the body, let me share the session I had with Betty.

Betty—Age 25

Betty came to see me to find out why she was not able to rid herself of a chronic lower back problem. She said she had experienced this problem her entire life. While she regularly went to a chiropractor for adjustments, she just ended up back where she started. The session revealed that her personality type is that of a caretaker and a worrier. Her energy system revealed that her personality weak site was her lower abdomen and lower back. Her caretaking patterns of behavior consistently drove her to want to care for the emotional needs of the people in her life. She was so driven by these patterns that she would take care of their needs before even thinking about taking care of her own. The emotional neediness of others burdened her, and she felt as if she were carrying everyone on her back.

Another personality pattern of behavior that Betty displayed was that of being a worrier. She worried about everything. In fact, worrying had become such a habit that there were times when she did not even know what she was worrying about. Betty worried about whether she would have enough energy to emotionally support those who needed it. She worried about whether she was doing a good job at work. She worried about whether she would have enough money to pay her bills even though she had gotten two pay raises in one year. She worried about being pulled in too many directions. She worried about having enough money to live on when she retired. Her worrying about retirement was interesting, since she was only 25 years old. I asked her about this, and she said the reason she was worrying was that her parents did not have enough retirement money and she had to carry them financially as well as herself.

All of the behavioral patterns associated with her personality type put her at risk for creating some kind of illness in her weak site. In fact, it was her worrying that was the root cause of her back problems—not surprising, since worry is a strong negative emotion and one that creates stress and chemical imbalance in the body. That chemical imbalance built up in her lower back and created so much muscle tension that her muscles were constantly pulling in opposite directions, thus putting pressure on the spine and causing it to continually be out of alignment. Her body finally reached a state physically and energetically where it could not carry any more and ended up creating chronic problems in the lumbar part of the spine. Interestingly enough, it was Betty's worrying about being pulled in different directions that her body responded to. It also became pulled in different directions and resulted in the lower back problem—another strong validation that the connection between personality and the human energy system affects how the mind and body communicate.

A *Shift in Thinking*

Partly due to current research findings, Western medicine is finally beginning to understand and embrace the idea that there is a connection between mind and body. Physicians are starting to recognize that in order to truly heal someone, they must deal with both the disease and the mental state of the person, and must treat the cause as well as the symptoms. More and more physicians are encouraging patients to see diagnosticians such as medical intuitives and holistic practitioners, who can help them understand how their patterns of behavior influence their health. These practitioners can also teach them how to change their thoughts, and modify destructive behavioral patterns that have the potential to create illness. While the processes that the practitioners use are not new or particularly innovative, more and more they are being proven effective. Some of these techniques include meditation, breathing exercises, visualization, and affirmations. These processes greatly improve a person's ability to control and channel their thoughts in a positive way, thus improving their physical health. The benefit of embracing this healing perspective and incorporating these techniques into our daily routines is that the root cause of the illness can be removed so that permanent healing can take place.

Your *Relationship with You*

I hope this chapter has helped to clarify which relationship may be the most important one you will ever build in your life. That is the relationship with yourself. As children, we are taught to focus our attention on building relationships with others and getting along with different people. We are encouraged to ignore others' quirks and idiosyncrasies and learn to live, love, and work with them. What we are not taught is how to love ourselves, how to look beyond our own quirks and imperfections, or how to change the habits we have formed that we do not like about ourselves or that tend to not serve us well.

I believe that through learning more about personality type, you can develop your own framework to better understand yourself. You will be able to recognize, comprehend, and utilize your personality strengths in such a way that you can maximize your innate capabilities and talents. You will have a deeper understanding of how your mind and body communicate, and you will become aware of where your weak site is. You will begin to recognize which thoughts and patterns of behavior are self-destructive and create chemical imbalances that increase your potential for illness.

At a deeper, more spiritual level, the understanding of your personality type positions you to give power to your individuality as expressed through the personality of your soul. You experience a sense of wholeness—the feeling of wholeness that only comes through the unconditional integration of body, mind, and spirit. Your true essence and authenticity will reveal itself through the lights of your aura for all to see and enjoy. You will experience the greatest, purest joy that there is in life—the joy that comes from accepting and loving yourself.

❦

Reflection

We are, to the world, a physical presence and a personality presence. We learn to deal with issues around our physical presence from the day we are born. Our personality presence impacts our lives to a great extent, and frequently we are oblivious of that impact.

❦   ❦   ❦

9

Color and Personality

"Color is inward and alive. Indeed the men of science tell us that it is an intense vibration, almost a quick pulsation of life itself."
— Vincent McNabb, author of *The Wayside*

The role that color plays in our lives is far more powerful than most of us may imagine. Color literally influences all aspects of who we are, both internally and externally. It affects us emotionally, psychologically, and physically, and its energy surrounds us and interpenetrates us. It resonates within us and emanates from us. It is as much a part of our daily existence as breathing, eating, and sleeping. The life force of energy we get from color is an integral component in our ability to maintain balance and stay healthy. In the human energy system, color serves as a vital communication link that reflects what is happening within all four layers of energy: spiritual, emotional, mental, and physical. It is through color or lack of it that a skilled intuitive can identify and classify illness in both the energy body and the physical body. For our energy system, color is food for the soul. It feeds our body, mind, and spirit.

While color does act as a perceptual stimulus, we can also simply enjoy its energy through our physical senses. We can bask in the warmth of the yellow rays of the sun; see beauty when we look at the red of a rose; and feel moved by the sight of clear blue skies, flaming orange sunsets, golden fields of wheat, green forests, and all of Earth's glorious colors. For the psyche, the beauty of color can inspire, uplift, and delight the human spirit. Emotionally, it can change our moods. It can provoke certain emotional responses and suppress others. It can make us blue, green with envy, or see red when angry. Color can stimulate or sedate, excite or calm. It can increase the temperature of the body, or it can make chills run up and down our spine. The effects that color has on us are innumerable, powerful, and very real.

Physically, the impact color has on the body, the endocrine system, and the autonomic nervous system is profound. For instance, red stimulates circulation, raises blood pressure, and creates a stress reaction that activates the release of adrenaline. It can create intestinal gas and constipation. The color orange aids in the digestive and metabolic systems by affecting how the pancreas and thyroid glands dialogue with each other. Yellow stimulates mental activity, activates motor nerves, and strengthens the cerebrospinal nervous system. Green heals and relaxes the body and stimulates activity in the heart and respiratory system. Basically, color can affect illness, the way the body repairs itself, mental and physical growth, and a person's overall state of health.

For decades, there has been interest in the effect that color has on our health. There have been numerous research studies that explore the important role color plays in the field of medicine in the prevention and treatment of illness. What these studies have revealed is that the perceptual response to specific colors is the same in every person. It makes no difference what their culture, personality type, or life circumstance is. The only time that this was not the case was with people who were color blind. It appears that our response to color is inherited and is a part of our neurological hardwiring. When we look at color, that color registers in the brain. The brain then sends an electrical message to the pituitary gland telling it how we are to react to the color it received. The pituitary gland, in turn, sends out a chemical message to the endocrine glands of the body, telling them which hormones to secrete, how much to secrete, and how that specific part of the body is to react.

An example of how color affects us took place in a research project conducted at the University of California, Berkeley, in 1979 for the California prison system. Guards who were considered to be in top physical condition were chosen to perform exercises using heavy dumbbells. They were instructed to do as many curling exercises as they could. After performing these exercises, a blue screen was put in front of them, blocking their view of anything else. Even though they felt tired, they were able to repeat the number of exercises. The blue color, while calming, acted in such a way that it allowed them to pace themselves better. Some even went on to exceed their previous number of repetitions. However, when a pink screen was placed in front of them, blocking their view of everything else, they all experienced a drastic reduction in the number of repetitions they could perform. Their muscles became fatigued, and they complained of being energetically drained. The impact was so severe that many were not even able to pick up the dumbbells. All their aggressiveness and competitiveness was gone. This research confirmed the premise that color does have a strong impact on us and can actually change the chemistry of the body. What this project pointed out is that pink slows down the circulation to the muscles and tranquilizes the body.

Linking Color to Personality

Looking at his research on the nature of personality, it's obvious that Carl Jung believed in the symbolic power of color. He would encourage his patients to use color spontaneously to help them express their personality. He believed that integrating color into their everyday lives would influence their behavior. It was, however, Dr. Max Luscher and his research that took color and applied it to the psychological functioning of personality type. Dr. Luscher believed that colors have an emotional value and that a person's reaction to color reveals their basic personality traits. His research provided conclusive evidence that specific colors create the same psychological, emotional, and physiological reaction in each person. While acknowledging that the measurement of emotions was not completely possible, he was able to measure the physical reaction of the body to specific colors. Working with the same premise that there are four different personality types, he developed a color test that could be used as a means of identifying the differences in people. What he learned about personality from the test results is that core personality preferences are organized into four color groups. The color name he gave to each group indicated the dominant organizing behavior around psychological functioning based on personality traits.

My own research delves even deeper into the relationship of color and personality and differs in some ways. The colors that I selected to represent the four personality types are representative of the totality of who we are. When I began looking at the predictable behavioral patterns found in personality type and connected those patterns of behavior to the psychological and emotional behavioral patterns associated with the four lower chakras of the human energy system, I discovered that they were inseparable. Then, taking the colors of the lower chakras—red, orange, yellow, and green—and looking at the psychological and physiological effects they have on the body, I again found that there was a consistent correlation. Working from that premise, I developed an interest in how all of these elements revealed themselves in the human energy system. What I discovered is that not only are they all connected, but they are interdependent upon each other. All influence our health, determine why we become ill, and identify the weak sites within the body.

Colors and Characteristics

Using Carl Jung's findings that psychological functioning falls into four categories: sensing, intuition, thinking, and feeling, I applied the four colors—red, orange, yellow, and green—of the chakra system to indicate the dominant organizing behavior or information-gathering process of each personality type. Here is what I discovered:

1. Red personality types are *sensing, thinking* in their functioning. Their orientation to the world is through external stimuli, and their core mental functioning is left brain. They are literal and see things as black or white. They are the most physical of all personalities and need to experience, to express, to do, and to achieve goals. They are hard working and ambitious people who are driven to conquer. With a traditional and conservative approach to life, they live more in the past than the present, and are concerned with personal safety and security. They are firm-minded, stubborn, and assertive, needing to control both their environment and the people in it. Inner conflict exists between the desire for power and status and the need to be left alone. Red energy stimulates all systems of the body. It represents aggression, passion, strength, and action. The color red excites and represents the blood of life.

2. Orange personality types are *sensing, feeling* in their functioning. Their orientation to the world is through people; thus they thrive on being able to fulfill the emotional needs of others. Their core mental functioning is left-right brain, so they make decisions based on how they feel about things. Orange energy seeks harmony and cooperation between people, and focuses on family and on the building of relationships that are mutually beneficial. They are emotional people and will use their emotions as a means of getting others to do what they want. They live more in the present than the past. Oranges become threatened when their security is jeopardized—they are jealous and protective of their things and the people they care about. They are worriers and have a fear of not having enough. They seek social acceptance. Orange energy is friendly, welcoming, and approachable. It is a social, warm color. The color orange relates to desire and ambition.

3. Yellow personality types are *intuitive, thinking* in their functioning. Their core mental functioning is right-left brain. However, the yellow personality type is the only one of the four that is mentally hard-wired to utilize all four of the psychological functions equally. They are both conceptual and analytical thinkers who pride themselves on their ability to solve problems—the more complex the better. They live in both the present and the future, experiencing time as a continuous flow of processes. They thrive on novelty and mental excitement, yet remain emotionally detached from people and situations. Their heightened sense of self and their need for independence and autonomy make them difficult to get to know. Yellow in the energy field reflects intellect and is a synthesis of both linear thinking and creativity. Its energy stimulates the mind. Yellow energy triggers creativity so one is stimulated to take on new challenges and explore new directions. Emotionally, from a positive perspective, yellow represents optimism and joy. Negatively, it represents lack of courage and fear of criticism.

4. Green personality types are *intuitive, feeling* in their functioning. Their orientation to the world is toward people and the need for relationships. Their core functioning is right-brained. They are expansive in their thinking—idea people who thrive on change and are constantly seeking new experiences. They are idealistic—they march to their own drummer, yet have a real need to fit in and find their community. They are continually hopeful and optimistic that they will find their place in society, since they need conflict-free environments and relationships, and are driven by their need to be liked. Greens seek energetic social contact and approval. They live in the past and future rather than in the present; consequently, they are seen as being disconnected from reality. They are continually impatient with the present because it is too slow to catch

up with their futuristic thinking. They have a deep long-
ing for spiritual fulfillment. In the human energy system,
green is the heart color; therefore, green personalities are
heart people. The color of wholeness, green energy promotes the balance of intuition with emotions. It represents the path to self-love and self-esteem. Physically, it
affects metabolism and acts as self-regulating energy for
the heart. Green acts as a stimulant to the respiratory system, encouraging us to breathe as a means of maintaining
balance, both physically and mentally. Energetically,
green acts as an antihistamine and decongestant to unclog
and remove blockages from within the energy body.

My work, as well as that of others, shows us that personality and
its psychological functions drive the way we think, how we act, and
why we develop the patterns of behavior we do. The four-color formula that I present to you in this book is a synthesis of all the different aspects of who you are: energetically, emotionally, mentally, and
physically. It is meant to provide a comprehensive model of looking
at yourself and guiding you toward a better understanding of what
you can do to have both a healthy personality and a healthy body. By
understanding what controls and directs you, you will be in a better
position to make the choices and changes in your life that move you
toward what you desire instead of repeating behavioral patterns that
prevent you from getting what you want. Your ability to heal yourself
rests largely upon knowing what you need to do to free yourself from
the patterns of behavior that can potentially lead to illness.

While I understand that there are risks and limitations that come
with categorizing people, the four-color formula is an effective way of
creating an awareness of the differences in people. It is not my intention to take away any person's individuality or uniqueness. It is, however, my intention to show you that while each of us is unique, we
still share common predictable patterns of behavior. I believe that
the four-color formula is a tool that can help us better understand the
complexity of human behavior and why we become ill.

The value of using color as a means of looking at personality is that it is nonthreatening. We all respond to color in much the same way, so it provides a basis for a common understanding. Besides, color is the universal language that bridges the physical and spiritual realms.

🦋

Reflection
There is a connection between the way our thinking processes work, and our personalities. That connection can be identified by a color, which ties directly to the colors of the four lower chakras.
Color then becomes an identifier of personality type, mental processing, behavioral tendencies, and wellness.

🦋 🦋 🦋

10

What Color Is Your Personality?

"To know thyself is the beginning of wisdom."
— Socrates

How can you tell your personality color or the personality colors of others if you are not able to see the energy field of the body? That question led me to develop the Personality Color Indicator (PCI) system. The PCI talks to the brain in such a way that it can be used as a means of identifying core personality traits that determine our psychological functioning, how we gather information, and how we draw conclusions or make decisions.

The PCI's primary purpose is to delineate the differences in behavioral patterns that are consistent from one personality type to another. The value of the PCI system is that it allows you to see yourself from a different perspective—the perspective of color. It is designed to provide a better understanding of why you think and act the way you do. The information that surfaces through the PCI can become the framework for you to better understand how to tap into and utilize your natural talents, strengths, and capabilities. Its information helps you explore the connection between your actual and perceived self so you can get a better sense of the direction you might take in your life. It brings forth valuable insight into the relationship you have with yourself and with others. It also provides an understanding of the differences in people and how those differences affect you.

What the Personality Color Indicator is not, is an instrument to determine the state of a person's mental health, the presence of personality disorders, a measurement of intelligence, or an evaluation of emotional stability. Like a mirror, it is simply a tool that provides a reflective approach to seeing yourself in a different way.

When looking at all the different aspects of personality, there are two other factors that should be at least discussed and taken into consideration. Those are the factors of introversion and extroversion, which influence how people interact and how they express themselves. They also impact how we first see people and how we energetically relate to them. While the PCI system does not identify these two factors in the assessment, I have included them in the type descriptions to show that two people can have the same personality color, and yet their introversion or extroversion factors can make them appear quite different. The reason for not including them in the assessment is that they do not directly impact the connection between personality, the energy system, and the chakras; also, they tend to change throughout the cycles we experience in life. The PCI system is only interested in core personality functioning and how that functioning affects the communication link between mind and body, and specifically the endocrine and nervous systems of the body.

While it is true that all of us are a little bit of each personality color, what I have discovered is that people cannot ignore or operate outside their core color for a prolonged period of time without experiencing a sense of confusion, energetic imbalance, or depletion—or without feeling an emotional detachment from themselves. Yes, we can change our color temporarily if circumstances or situations demand. However, we must first operate from the way we are genetically wired before we can successfully or satisfactorily experience the qualities of another color. The way our body will tell us if we are operating outside our core functioning and strengths is that we will experience a strong stress reaction, and we will not be able to sustain clarity of thought.

Each of us can develop more flexibility in our color by learning how to recognize and change the habits that keep us locked into repeating old patterns of behavior. Once we develop flexibility, we can work on expanding our mental functioning in such a way that we fully utilize a whole-brain approach. We can consciously draw on the different aspects of who we are for a specific purpose such as healing. We can turn our weaknesses into strengths. And, we can grow beyond our self-perceived limitations and find balance, harmony, happiness, and success in our lives.

The Personality Color Indicator

The PCI identifies predominant personality traits and characteristics. It will classify those differences into four color categories: *red, orange, yellow,* and *green.* The best approach to take when making your choices is to act on your first instinctive response. Avoid becoming analytical or subjective, and do not make your choices based on how you want others to see you. Keep in mind that there are no right or wrong choices.

Instructions: *Read each statement carefully. If you agree with the statement or believe that it represents your most frequent and habitual patterns, circle the letter to its left. If you do not agree, go on to the next statement.*

A 1. I consider myself to be down-to-earth.

A 2. I prefer to stick to a set daily routine rather than put myself in unfamiliar situations.

B 3. I enjoy using my creativity to come up with innovative ways of doing things rather than doing them the way that everyone else does.

A 4. I stay focused and concentrate on what needs to be completed now rather than thinking about future tasks.

B 5. I become bored with tasks that are repetitious and find myself looking for different and better methods of doing them.

B 6. I enjoy the challenge of finding solutions to problems that are complex and that need to be explored from a variety of perspectives.

A 7. I consider myself to be practical, not theoretical.

B 8. I have a lot of thoughts in my head simultaneously, and I am often accused of not listening or of being preoccupied.

A 9. I would rather work with facts and figures than theories and ideas.

B 10. I pride myself on using my intellect and being a creative problem solver.

A 11. I would rather deal with the known than explore possibilities.

B 12. I prefer being original rather than traditional.

B 13. I am interested in how machines and products work so I can come up with ways to improve them.

B 14. I prefer learning new skills more than using old ones.

A 15. I am detail oriented.

A 16. I find myself attracted to people who are similar to me: realistic, practical, and involved with current issues.

A 17. I become impatient and frustrated with problems or tasks that are too complicated.

B 18. I prefer to read books that provoke thought and allow the mind to wander and explore a variety of scenarios.

A 19. I would rather follow standard operating procedures than create new ways of doing things.

A 20. I want work tasks and time expectations clearly defined before I begin a project.

B 21. I am usually on a different wavelength from most people.

B 22. I tend to answer questions with a question in order to gather more information.

A 23. I interpret things literally rather than conceptually.

A 24. I am more interested in the production and distribution of products than in their design and application.

B 25. I thrive on variety and dislike repetition.

B 26. I am a risk-taker and shun the conservative approach to life.

A   27. I look for tried and proven ways to solve problems and rely on past experiences rather than wasting my time seeking new and unproven solutions.

B   28. I enjoy listening to new ideas and exploring their potential rather than dealing with the mundane.

B   29. I would rather create with my mind than produce with my hands.

A   30. When confronted with a problem, I react quickly rather than dwelling on it before doing anything.

D   31. I will suppress my own feelings rather than hurt the feelings of others.

D   32. I go overboard for people and overextend myself to meet their needs, even at my own expense.

C   33. I do not show my feelings easily and have been told that I am hard to get to know.

C   34. I would rather deal with task problems than people problems.

C   35. I resolve conflicts based on what is fair rather than being concerned with feelings.

D   36. I find that people tend to take advantage of my good nature and kindheartedness.

C   37. I react with logic rather than emotion.

C   38. I make decisions based on logic rather than emotions.

C   39. I rarely seek advice from others before I make a decision.

D   40. I warm up to people easily and would not want to be thought of as cold and indifferent.

D   41. I prefer a work environment where there is no conflict and where people are appreciated and praised for what they contribute.

C   42. I am critical by nature and express my opinions freely.

D   43. I show my feelings easily.

D   44. I am accepting of others, not judgmental.

D   45. I expect those close to me to be sensitive to my feelings and emotional ups and downs, and I feel hurt when they are not.

D 46. I resolve conflicts by asking people for their advice so that I can gain reassurance and confidence in my decisions.

C 47. I stay calm, cool, and collected in situations where others are reacting emotionally.

D 48. I am good at resolving people problems.

C 49. I am a perfectionist and like things done the right way— my way.

C 50. I am more task oriented than people oriented.

D 51. I am more concerned with making *good* decisions than *right* decisions.

C 52. I would rather work with someone who is reasonable and responsible than with someone who is thoughtful and kind.

D 53. I am a peacemaker, not an aggressor.

D 54. I tend to be overly sympathetic to the needs of people.

C 55. I am more interested in solving problems than dwelling on them.

C 56. I deal with people issues in a straightforward manner and call them like they are.

D 57. It is important to promote good feelings and harmony within my relationships.

C 58. I think that it is more important to be respected than to be liked.

D 59. I am good at creating a team atmosphere and getting others to rally around a common goal or cause.

C 60. I show how much I care for someone by being responsible and conscientious rather than being emotional and sentimental.

Total the letters circled:

    A_____   B_____   C_____   D_____

Add **A** and **C** together.
Add **B** and **C** together.
Add **A** and **D** together.
Add **B** and **D** together.

RED   YELLOW

A + C _____   B + C _____

ORANGE   GREEN

A + D _____   B + D _____

Your highest numerical score denotes your predisposition for that particular color type. If your score is particularly high in your color type, it indicates that you are strongly influenced by the characteristics and patterns of behavior associated with that type. If your numbers are close, they indicate flexibility within your type. It is not unusual if your color type is *green* to have numbers very close in more than one other color, because *greens* are the chameleons of the personality world. It is also not unusual for *green* and *orange* numbers to be close. The reason for this is that both make decisions based on emotions. The same holds true for *reds* and *yellows*, since both make decisions based on logic. Also, please note that your numerical scores may change depending on what is happening in your life. However, your strongest color type will remain consistent no matter what challenges life places on your path.

Note: *Each of us regularly uses all of the mental processes identified in the Personality Color Indicator. However, we do not use all of them equally well. The objective of the PCI system is to identify your preferred core personality traits as they relate to your information-gathering and decision-making processes.*

Please remember that no color is better or worse than any other. Use the information that surfaces through the PCI as a tool to help you better understand who you are and how you relate to others. Using this information as a foundation to build from, you can strengthen your innate qualities and readjust the behavioral patterns that both prevent you from getting what you want, and affect your health in a negative way. My greatest desire is that you will use this information as a way of learning how to appreciate and accept the differences in people. Just keep in mind that your weakness may be someone else's strength. And that, collectively, those differences can create mutually beneficial relationships.

🐝

Reflection
Our core personality traits define who we are,
how we gather information, and how we make decisions.
In this complex world of family, social, casual,
and work-related interactions with people,
we are constantly reminded that
we are not all the same.

The first step in recognizing that there are differences
is to understand why those differences exist.
The second step is to accept that differences are just that—
differences—nothing more, nothing less.

🐝   🐝   🐝

11

The Red Personality

"Red stirs the senses and passions."
— Dr. Morton Walker, author of *The Power of Color*

The words that best describe *reds* are *practical, realistic, down-to-earth, sensible, pragmatic,* and *dependable*. Traditionalist in their beliefs and values, *reds* are the backbone of society. They believe that people should earn their way in life through hard work and service to others. Rigidly conscientious, they approach everything from a no-nonsense point of view. *Reds* see the world for exactly what it appears to be—what you see is what you get. Loyal to their families, their causes, and their superiors, they operate best within traditional power structures where everyone knows their place. They are sensitive to lines of authority and are rigid about staying within those lines. Even if *reds* do not agree with rules or procedures, they will not challenge them. They accept them for what they are and understand that without structure and guidelines, there would be chaos.

Reds are masters at managing the everyday realities of life. They do what needs to be done, moving ahead even when resources are limited. Their motto is "Get it done, don't make excuses, and learn to work with what you have." Once *reds* set their minds to doing something, they refuse to be distracted by people and problems that might impede their progress. They believe that there are specific ways in which things should be done. And, to ensure that things are done their way, they will create rules and expect others to follow them. *Reds*, by nature, are not risk takers, and if they must take risks, it will be only after careful consideration. They prefer to act on what they know, and stay with the tried and true rather than doing something for the first time or doing something that has never been done before. Their world is tangible. If you cannot see it, hear it, touch it, taste it, or smell it, then it is not real. Binary in their approach to life, they see a right way and a wrong way and nothing in between. They need tasks and projects well defined; otherwise, they become stressed and feel out of control. They are most comfortable in relationships and environments where they are in control and know what is going on at all times.

Reds are rapid-fire thinkers and become impatient with too much planning. They set concrete objectives and work hard to reach those objectives as quickly and directly as possible. They do not see value in analyzing a situation to death, preferring to act and get things done. *Reds* are literal in their interpretation of things—everything is black or white. Gray areas and ambiguity are not comfortable for them; intangibles have very little value in a *red's* world. For them, spending time exploring possibilities and creating ideas that are nonproductive or that may not go anywhere is a total waste of time. They are not abstract thinkers and, in fact, have very little patience for people who are. This is not to say that they are not idea people—they are, but unless they have some assurance that the idea will work prior to moving forward, they will view it as a waste of time, and wasting time does not sit well with them. *Reds* see their role in the creative process as that which gives it substance and turns ideas into reality.

Reds have a need to control—both their environment and the people in it. They believe that if they are in control, then they can somehow buffer themselves from life's surprises, which they so dislike. They do not give compliments easily, believing instead that people must earn them. *Reds* tend to focus on what is wrong with people rather than focusing on their positive qualities. They are known for berating others for their negative behavior and yet not ever seeing their own behavior as negative. Autocratic and dictatorial in their interaction with others, they are highly effective at using intimidation and aggression in order to get what they want. Their need to dominate is so strong that they are often accused of being insensitive to the feelings and needs of others; however, that is not the case. *Reds* see their domination of others as a means of teaching, of helping them to be better. They see others who think differently as difficult to get along with or simply argumentative. They are strong, forceful personalities who are driven by the need for power and status.

Reds are fiercely competitive. In their rush to win, they may simply push others aside or run over them. They will not back down from a confrontational situation, seeing compromise as defeat. They thrive in competitive environments and use competition as a means of motivation. *Reds* view themselves as survivalists. For them, winning is everything—no matter how high the price or how demanding the conditions, they will not be squeamish in their quest for winning or being on top. If winning means stepping on others to get what they want, then so be it. They do not identify with the underdogs nor do they have a need to feel sorry for them. From the *red* perspective, there can only be one winner, and that winner will be them. In their reality, the more challenging or ferocious the competition, the more stimulating it is. They prefer taking the offensive position rather than the defensive or passive position.

Hard work is the hallmark of *reds*—they make things happen. Driven by a need for completion, they will not rest until the job is done; only then can they justify time off to play. They work hard and play hard, rolling up their sleeves and jumping right in. *Reds* pride themselves on their ability to manage people, deal with facts, and solve problems. They are detail oriented, and for them, no detail is too small to overlook. They need structure in both their lives and work, and they are happiest working in environments where systems and procedures are well established. They need all tasks and expectations to be well defined and do not like wasting time. *Reds* are the kinds of employees that every employer dreams of—loyal, steadfast, and dependable, they do not mind taking on routine or redundant tasks. They become resentful and feel their time is being wasted in meetings where there is no agenda, or that are open ended. Being involved in conversations that are not going anywhere is a major thorn in their side. *Reds* do not work well in environments where they have to guess at what needs to be done; rather, they need to know precisely what their tasks and responsibilities are, and how their performance is going to be measured. They need others to tell them what, when, and why. They do not like to fill in the blanks because someone else forgot to tell them everything. Needing to see immediate results from their efforts, their motto in life is, "Just do it."

Since *reds* are hard workers, they expect the same of others. They have little tolerance for people who make excuses or who are nonproductive, expecting people to keep their personal problems to themselves, and to definitely leave them at home. The work environment is no place for emotional issues. They measure on the bottom line, expect results, and do not place value merely on effort. They believe that everything depends on them, and that it is their responsibility to drive others to get things done. *Reds* will never be accused of being freeloaders, because they believe in earning their way. They have a strong work ethic and believe in giving a good day's work for a good day's pay.

Reds see what they do for a living as the means of identifying who they are because they live to work and work to live. Their work offers them the greatest opportunity to utilize and capitalize on their strengths. Job titles are important to *reds* because their titles let others know how successful they are. *Reds* who do not have (or believe they do not have) important titles or important jobs tend to suffer from low self-esteem. Their self-confidence level seems to be directly tied to their work and their position. For a *red* to be out of work is extremely uncomfortable and destructive to their overall confidence level, and being vulnerable creates anxiety and paranoia. Their need to provide for their families is so strong that when they are unable to fulfill these responsibilities, they become frustrated, angry, and prone to deep states of depression.

Reds want to belong and to serve. They need that consistency in their lives and relationships and do not like change unless they initiate it. They are driven by their sense of responsibility to provide the basic human necessities for their families, such as food, shelter, and clothing. They are firm believers in the need for rules that govern the interaction of people, whether they relate to family, work, city, school, or church. They are staunch disciplinarians, and their path in life is that of duty and dedication. They are drawn to jobs that are predictable and offer long-term security.

Reds are physical people. They are aggressive, active, rough-and-tumble individuals. They are physically assertive and enjoy participating in activities that involve physical contact. They tend to make good leaders because they know what it takes to get the job done. They also understand what it takes to make a good team and are not shy about pushing people to get the best performance out of them. They pursue life with gusto, vitality, and courage. They want to be involved in the game of life and are never comfortable sitting on the sidelines. The more intense and focused the activities, the happier they are. *Reds* will be the first to roll up their sleeves and dive into a project if the rewards are great enough.

At their best, *reds* are production machines. They are consistent in their behavior and are seen by others as the driving forces of progress. Once *reds* understand what needs to be done, get out of their way. They will bulldoze anything in their paths and are tireless in the pursuit of getting the job done. *Reds* will not sit around twiddling their thumbs waiting for others to make decisions. If things are going too slow for *reds*, they will provide whatever motivation is necessary to make things happen. Their greatest ability is to solve problems by the collection and assimilation of facts. Their mental processing is sequential and orderly. They believe in taking one step at a time, never making educated guesses. Methodical and painstaking in their attention to detail, *reds* look at all of the facts and base their decisions on those facts and historical precedent. If the facts substantiate their decision, then that decision becomes cast in concrete.

At their worst, *reds* are indecisive, overly cautious, abrupt, and argumentative. They become so focused on what is directly in front of them that they lose sight of any long-range view. They cannot see the forest for the trees. They are known to resolve problems too quickly just to get them out of their hair. If pressed to make a decision without what they consider adequate information, they become frustrated and contentious. They feel like they are out of control and consequently become rigid and resistant to any input from others. They just want to be left alone. Life becomes depressing, and reality becomes their worst nightmare. They become moody and pessimistic. Their need to control drives them to want to dominate others even more. That domination pushes others even farther away, leaving *reds* feeling isolated and unloved. At their very worst, *reds* play "poor me." They want others to feel sorry for them because they work so hard and carry so much of the burden of life. *Reds* can get so caught up in feeling sorry for themselves that they lose touch with reality. They become inefficient and nonproductive. When in this state of mind, *reds* see life as just one unpleasant thing after another. They become dissatisfied with everything and everyone. If really feeling out of control, *reds* become paranoid and think that everyone is out to get them or take what they have.

Extroverted Reds

Extroverted *reds* believe in making the most of the moment. They are doers who like to keep themselves involved in life. They like to keep things lively and churning as much as possible. This behavior keeps others off balance so *reds* feel like they are in control. Even though *reds* do not like change, they are known for changing direction midstream just to keep people on their toes. They do not rest on their laurels, and they make things happen however they need to. If extroverted *reds* decide that something needs to get done, either join in the effort and match their pace, or get out of their way.

They are impatient and have difficulty relaxing if there are things that need to be done. Extroverted *reds* do not cope well with things that do not go their way. They need to control the activities and agenda. You either go along or you don't go at all.

Reds are outgoing, gregarious, straightforward, extremely direct, and vocal when it comes to expressing what they like or do not like. They do not pull any punches when it comes to telling others what they want and expect. They are masters at getting to the heart of matters. When they ask questions, they expect simple, direct answers. They have no tolerance for lengthy, complex explanations. If they ask you the time, give them only the time. They do not want to know how the watch was built.

Introverted Reds

Introverted *reds* are quiet, introspective, serious, matter-of-fact, reserved people who are reliable and steadfast. They are patient and painstakingly systematic in their approach to solving problems. Unlike their extroverted counterparts, they will not exert themselves any more than they have to. They do not enter into things impulsively. They do not see bulldozing ahead or butting heads with people as a good use of their time or energy. They are methodical in their approach to both life and tasks. To them, life is what you see and nothing more. No other types are more thorough, hardworking, or patient than introverted *reds*. Their perseverance and quiet presence tends to act as a stabilizer for others. They will not do anything that does not make sense. They enjoy quiet activities and solitude and prefer working by themselves rather than working with people. For introverted *reds*, people and their problems are distractions. They need a life that will give them the stability they need without emotional demands.

Reflection
*The red's world is one of hard work, realism,
compliance, and stability.*

*Imagine an automobile, and the part of it that each personality type
would identify with. The red would be the motor and the driveline—
the parts of the auto that power it to make it go. Reds move the world.*

❦ ❦ ❦

12

The Orange Personality

"Orange is the social color of service to mankind."
— Alex Jones, author of *Seven Mansions of Color*

Orange personalities are, by nature, caretakers. Caring for and about other people is what makes their lives worth living. Both men and women are especially attuned to the basic needs of the people in their lives, and will always put the needs of others before their own. You will not find another type who is more loving, more solicitous, more sensitive, or more concerned about basic human emotional needs than an *orange*. They are devoted and committed to those they care about, and of all types they are the most family-oriented—both to their blood families and to their work families. *Oranges* will instinctively assume the role of caretakers and they take this responsibility very seriously. They work hard to maintain a balanced, comfortable, and emotionally nurturing environment. They feel it is their responsibility to do everything for other people so those people will be happy.

A good way to describe *oranges* is as mother hens, always wanting to protect their chicks. As the mother hen, they tuck their chicks under their wings until the chicks are strong and old enough to venture out on their own. *Oranges* fret and worry about the well-being of those they care about. They tend to make excuses for others and defend them. They see their role as that of the peacemaker.

At their best, *oranges* are devoted, considerate, and ever-so-helpful team players. For *oranges*, it makes no difference whether the team is family, work, church, a charitable organization, or the military. They have a strong sense of community and need to be involved in activities that will directly benefit themselves and those they care about. Crusaders who champion the rights of those less fortunate, they are socially responsible and expect others to be the same. *Oranges* bring a sense of tradition and provide good solid values, knowing that both of these are necessary to build a foundation for a strong, healthy society. Their lives focus on doing what is right and what is conventional. To *oranges*, the soundness of any good idea is not judged by the individual who created it, but by the outside community where it will positively affect the lives of others. It is not uncommon to find *oranges* in leadership capacities in either community projects or organizations if they believe their involvement will have an impact.

However, they are not always leaders on the job. They are dutiful and willing to relinquish authority if need be, always willing to help others. Since they are team players, their needs are the same as those of the group leader, and their happiness comes from the fulfillment of the directives and goals of others. What *oranges* will do in most workplaces is position themselves so they become the hub of information, and others will rely on them. When *oranges* do take the leadership position, they make things happen by gaining the cooperation and support of others. They are natural administrators and make task management look easy. They are skilled at communicating the tasks that are necessary to get the job done, and at communicating in such a way that people freely cooperate and join in. *Oranges* expect and require others to be considerate of feelings and become dismayed when they are not. If others let them down, *oranges* feel taken advantage of and betrayed and react strongly. Then these usually polite, courteous people become very aggressive and outspoken.

Oranges love to bring people together. Social types, they seem to make friends wherever they go. They enjoy entertaining—to an *orange* it is an event, and they are willing to do things that will make other people feel at home, such as fixing favorite dishes for their guests. They have a personal flair that is unique to their own type when entertaining. They entertain with one thought in mind, to make it fun for everyone involved. If you get invited to an *orange's* party, you can be sure that you will feel pampered. They love theme parties. For example, if an *orange* throws a Hawaiian party, not only will the food conform to the theme, but so will the decorations and the attire. Their attention to detail in party planning goes beyond what most would think of. *Oranges* are masters at creating an atmosphere where people can escape the realities of day-to-day life. As hosts, they are considerate of dietary needs, seeing that their guests are comfortable and that everyone is involved in the conversations and activities, and always anticipating the needs of their guests. They believe the way to people's hearts is through caring and making life as enjoyable as possible. *Oranges*, while being somewhat serious by nature, know that laughter and the ability to laugh is the best medicine. They are good at making others laugh but often forget to laugh themselves.

Oranges are extremely sensitive to the feelings of others. They are good listeners, so others will seek them out to share their feelings and emotional hurts. *Oranges* have a knack for sorting out complex emotional problems and emotionally volatile situations. They are natural counselors. If you ever want to take a pulse of the emotional level in an environment, especially at work, talk to an *orange*. They make it their business to know where people are emotionally. You can always count on an *orange* to get a clear picture of people's attitudes, their likes and dislikes, who is having an emotional trauma, and who is not. *Oranges* are committed to creating a productive, harmonious environment, be it at work or at home.

Oranges are naturally cautious and approach any kind of change with trepidation until they fully understand the implications and the impact the change will have on their lives, security, and family. *Oranges*, if given a choice, will never jeopardize themselves or those they love by taking unnecessary risks through reckless actions or careless thinking. *Oranges* are worriers. Consequently, they work very hard at trying to always be prepared. They will worry about anything and everything. They tend to live with a constant low-level anxiety about life and a vague apprehension that leaves them wary and overly cautious. Their first tendency will always be to stay within familiar comfort zones rather than taking risks or trying something new. They will procrastinate or postpone having to deal with change until they have time to see how it feels. If it feels right and they think it is in their best interests, they will not only embrace the changes, but they will make the changes work for the good of everyone.

Oranges like their homes and their work environment to be tidy and orderly. Interestingly enough, an *orange* will accept disarray in others' lives but not in their own. *Oranges* can only handle disarray for a short period of time and then they become compelled to "get their house in order." Being out of order makes them moody and difficult to be around. They become depressed, show signs of frustration, and become emotionally agitated. This behavior is contradictory to their nature and is negative and destructive for them. When *oranges* are functioning effectively, they are competent and thorough. They are hardworking, patient, and extremely productive. They can move mountains if necessary to get things done. When functioning ineffectively, they are self-absorbed, stubborn, and brooding. They allow things to fall between the cracks. They start feeling sorry for themselves and wallow in self-pity. They will lash out and blame others for what is happening. To them, it is rarely their fault.

Oranges are courteous people unless crossed. It takes a lot to push an *orange* to the point where they will lash out at others, but when they do, there is no doubt in anyone's mind that the *orange* has reached their limit. When crossed, *oranges* become rigid and stubborn and express their emotional hostility vehemently. They lash out and use words that create instant anxiety and shock in others. When *oranges* unleash their rage, it will usually catch others so off guard that they will feel like a deer caught in headlights, about to get hit. If feeling pressed, *oranges* will become extremely temperamental, and emotionally fly off the handle at every little thing. Their emotional outbursts cause others to seriously question if they want be around them. At their worst, *oranges* become cynical, negative, and back-stabbing, and if they are feeling insecure, their behavior becomes erratic. *Oranges*, when stressed, are demanding. They hold grudges and do not easily forgive and forget. The best way to deal with *oranges* when they are in this mind-set is to allow them to get their feelings off their chests and then leave them alone for a while. This allows them time to reconcile their feelings with both their guts and their minds.

Oranges have a strong need for personal praise—even though when praised, they will usually respond by saying, "It was nothing." Constant and tangible signs of reassurance is what gives *oranges* a sense of self-worth and self-confidence. They need to know they are appreciated and are an integral part of the team. With *oranges*, a simple, "job well done," will keep them motivated and productive. *Oranges* are always inquiring either directly or indirectly about others' feelings, office politics, or what is currently going on in people's lives. Keeping a finger on daily activities helps them feel secure and alleviates most of the fears they have of being left out or missing something that will have a direct impact on their security.

Oranges are careful to promote good feelings between themselves and the people who are important in their lives. They are polite, agreeable, and tactful. They are interested in creating environments that will encourage people to be productive. They will usually create committees to deal with issues. They are always looking for ways to involve people as the means of making things happen. They will try to solve problems by working to understand the perspectives of the people involved. They will hold private meetings with those involved in order to obtain thé vital data necessary to make decisions. *Oranges* use this process so they can get a clear picture of how decisions will affect the group collectively. They are sympathetic toward the personal problems of others.

Oranges dislike conflict and will work hard to avoid it. However, unlike their emotional counterparts, *greens*, they will not shy away from it, even if it requires compromising their traditional values or time with their families. *Oranges* more than any other type struggle with the balance between work and home. On the one hand, they are loyal employees and take their jobs seriously, and on the other hand, they are driven by the needs of their family. *Oranges* are willing to work hard and put in long hours if that is what is required to get the job done. But do not expect them to make a habit of it.

Oranges also tend to be physical people, but they are not driven competitively, as are *reds*. Where *reds* will bulldoze their way forward no matter what, *oranges* understand their limits and the boundaries of those limitations. Instead of pushing forward head-on into obstacles, they will listen to what their gut tells them. They will step back and evaluate what price they will have to pay to accomplish the desired results. If the results do not justify the risk to them or to those they care about, they will back away. *Reds'* interpretation of this type of behavior is that *oranges* are not committed. The truth is that *oranges* are just more sensitive.

Oranges manage their resources well and plan for the future. For them, having money means that they can make the choices they want in life. They believe that financial stability is their only security. They enjoy the accumulation of material possessions. They plan for retirement so they will not have to worry about their security. They want to be able to help their children and to send them to good schools. *Oranges* are frugal and save money throughout their lives. It is important to them to make sure their financial resources will be sufficient when they retire so they can continue to live a comfortable lifestyle. They want to have flexibility to do as they please and go where they want. When you ask *oranges* what they plan to do when they retire, it will usually involve some kind of community activity that will benefit others, such as volunteering.

An *orange's* self-esteem is directly tied to and influenced by the quality of their relationships. Their emotional stability is based on how others react and interact with them. *Oranges* more than any other type are the most concerned with making a good impression. They work hard to gain the appreciation of others. Once *oranges* know they are loved and appreciated, then their emotional anxieties are relieved and their caretaking qualities can shine.

Self-control is not usually a problem for an *orange*. However, when they are experiencing difficulties in their relationships, they have a tendency toward addictions such as eating disorders, and alcohol and substance abuse. *Oranges* struggle deeply with having to cope with problems that are emotional in nature and/or threaten their security. The behavioral pattern for *oranges* in this situation is to create an abundance of petty problems so they will not have to deal with real issues. If they feel that the problem is more than they can emotionally handle, they suffer from depression or become physically ill.

Extroverted Oranges

Extroverted *oranges* are warm, friendly, good-natured, and charming types. They bring humor to situations and enjoy events and activities that encourage laughter and jovial interaction. They tend to view life as an eternal cornucopia from which flows an endless supply of sensual-aesthetic experiences.

Working with an extroverted *orange* is rarely dull. They are friendly motivators who look for ways to make work more fun even though they work diligently. They add zip to the workplace and are the caretakers of the office social calendar. They will plan Christmas parties, birthday parties, employee farewells, employee-recognition events, and contests. They manage the details of these events with great ease.

Extroverted *oranges* tend to overextend themselves. Since they make handling details and people look so easy and seem to be so skilled at juggling a multitude of tasks, others come to expect this from them. Instead of saying no, an *orange* will just keep on going and doing until they run themselves into the ground. They have a difficult time pacing themselves. They are so driven by the need to be appreciated and considered a valuable part of the team that they forget they can run out of energy. Extroverted *oranges* are binary—either happy or sad. They are either going full speed ahead or are down for the count.

Introverted Oranges

Quiet, friendly, responsible, and *conscientious* describes an introverted *orange*. They are painstakingly thorough and accurate. They are patient with details and work steadily to get the job done. As with their extroverted counterparts, it is important for them to be part of the team. However, as with the introverted *reds*, they prefer to work alone. They are modest about their organizational skills and abilities and would rather be loyal followers than leaders. If you were to look behind the scenes of every great leader, you would most likely find an introverted *orange* who is seeing that things get done.

Introverted *oranges* do not enter into activities impulsively. Once they do get involved, they are extremely focused and hard to distract. They do not quit easily and will stay committed to the project or tasks at hand until the job is done.

They are intensely private people. They find it difficult to express themselves and tend to hold things inside. Actually, all they are doing is observing and listening so they can determine if the person is someone who they want to include in their relationship network. Introverted *oranges* are very selective about whom they choose to share their time, energy, and feelings with.

🐜

Reflection
The orange's world is filled with caretaking of family, friends, co-workers, associates, and neighbors—anyone who has a need. Oranges are realistic and down-to-earth people.

Relating to the automobile, the orange would be the body and the windows, sheltering and protecting the occupants, keeping them safe and secure.

🐜 🐜 🐜

13

The Yellow Personality

"Yellow is the color of intellect, innovation, and the love for things that are contemporary and challenging."
— Faber Birren

Yellows are self-confident personalities. The "self" words that best describe *yellows* are *self-reliant, self-made, self-respected, self-motivated, self-starting,* and *self-fulfilled. Yellows* believe in themselves, their capabilities, and their intellectual abilities. They know that if they put their minds to it, they can accomplish anything. Their philosophy is that if they can conceive it, they can achieve it. When you add in the *yellow* characteristic of ambition, you realize that they truly are capable of transforming their dreams into real accomplishments. To *yellows,* the future is a world of endless possibilities and the opportunity to make a difference. *Yellows* are true visionaries.

Yellows are natural leaders who instinctively move to the helm. They have a leadership persona that lets others know they are capable of taking charge. Their leadership style is evident in all of their relationships: family, friends, work, and community. However, it is the work environment that provides *yellows* the greatest opportunity to bring their gifts and talents for leadership to their greatest fruition. In fact, *yellows* are most capable of reaching their true potential when they are in charge. They enjoy the challenges that come with taking on the leadership role. They are at ease and confident in assuming enormous responsibilities. Consequently, others are glad to have *yellows* step forward, make the tough decisions, and deal with problems and obstacles. Except for *reds*, most people find it comforting to have someone they can depend on who will be their protector, someone who is willing to stand up and speak out, someone they know they can trust and rely on, and see as a competent leader. The relationship between *reds* and *yellows* can be highly competitive because each thinks they should be in the leadership position.

Yellows are challengers. Critical and opinionated, they challenge the way things are done, and they challenge authority. They challenge the traditional ways of thinking, and they challenge why and how things work. They even challenge themselves to be better and to think differently. Their motto is "Think out of the box." They are conceptual thinkers and see the big picture, so they are not bound by the same mental restrictions or emotional fears that limit other personality types. *Yellows* dare to do things differently and strive to make things better. They are always looking for ways to build a better mousetrap. *Yellows* are nonconformists and are seen as mavericks. For other personality types, *yellows* are often seen as loose cannons, doing what they want without giving thought to how things have been done in the past, or as dreamers who have their heads in the clouds. This is not the case; *yellows* have a very clear vision of where they are going. They just do not always find it necessary to tell others. They are analytical thinkers and are very strategic in their planning. Once they determine the best way that something should be done, then they move forward without distraction.

Yellows struggle throughout their lives trying to conform to the rules of society. They are truly square pegs trying to fit into a round world. *Yellows* live by their own internal code of values and principles. They are not strongly influenced by other people or by traditional limitations. They have their own game plan as to what they think their life should be and what they should accomplish. They are tenacious people and have true grit. *Yellows* are courageous in their thinking and will not back down if they believe something is not right. Their creativity comes from their capacity for deep thinking. They speculate endlessly about the what and why before making their decisions. When bogged down in their thinking, they may suffer from analysis paralysis. *Yellows* enjoy a good debate and will not retreat from a stimulating conversation or a sparring match of words and thoughts. They enjoy the opportunity to change the perspective and thinking of others.

Yellows, like *reds*, are competitive personalities. However, unlike *reds*, where winning is everything, *yellows* will not compete against anyone they think is inferior to them in either thinking or skills. For *reds*, being competitive means winning. In contrast, the kind of competition that stimulates *yellows* is the kind where they are competing against someone they view as a formidable competitor and where the outcome will be meaningful to them. *Yellows* must compete against someone they respect, someone they can learn from, or someone who they view as their peer or competitive superior. *Yellows* will not seek out those who they believe they can readily beat. In these situations, winning is not meaningful. In fact, for *yellows*, competition must fill an ego need. Otherwise, it wastes their time.

Yellows need the freedom to utilize their intelligence, to pursue their quest for knowledge and wisdom, and to develop competency by acquiring new skills and expanding their capabilities. For *yellows*, being competent and a self-acknowledged expert is most important. They will not settle for anything less. They pride themselves on their expertise and intellect. They view life as something to be understood and mastered. Research is their forte. They make great researchers because of their need to understand, predict, and explain both concept and reality. They are compulsive about improving things. For *yellows*, knowing how something works is only half the equation. Knowing how to make it better is the other half.

Yellows are idea people who have the capability of turning ideas into reality. For *yellows*, ideas are merely solutions to problems. Instead of dwelling on problems, they focus on solving them. For *yellows*, problems are opportunities to learn, flex their intellectual capabilities, and challenge their skills. They are cerebral people who are multisensory in the way they see things. Their sixth sense is an integral part of their mental functioning. They approach thinking from a logical perspective, trusting and using their five senses to supply the needed information and then crossing over to access their intuitive insights to provide all of the possible scenarios. For *yellows*, exploring concepts, possibilities, and ideas is stimulating. They are happiest when they are being challenged mentally and when they must assimilate and manipulate information. They need to be allowed to have the time to work through the information the way they are mentally programmed. If they do not, they become resentful and unwilling to make decisions.

Yellows are overly critical, authoritarian, and can be arrogant personalities. They are driven by the need for perfection from both themselves and others. To *yellows*, there is only one way to do things and that is their way. *Yellows* are the most self-critical of all the personalities. They will badger themselves about their errors in judgment. They are ruthless in monitoring their own progress, and they never need others to point out their shortcomings. They do it themselves. *Yellows* do not need critics; they can be their own worst critic. For *yellows*, to obtain what they perceive as perfection, they are constantly evaluating, analyzing, and escalating their standards. What is accepted by *yellows* as a satisfactory performance one day may only be adequate the next. And, being "just adequate" is viewed as missing the mark. They have very high standards of excellence. Their drive for perfection creates a constant low-level anxiety of self-doubt within themselves. The greatest challenge for *yellows* is to learn how to trust both their logic and their emotions. Trusting emotions is not something they do instinctively or easily. This is not to say that they are not emotionally sensitive people, because they are; they just do not use their emotions to make decisions, nor do they show them readily to others.

Yellows are planners and organizers. They are masters at designing and perfecting systems and procedures to get the best results. If they were going on a trip, they would plan the whole thing out in such detail that they could tell you precisely how long the trip is, what to expect the weather to be, and what clothing to take, anticipating all possible scenarios. They would verify all of the reservations well in advance of departure. They would be able to tell you what activities are available, which geographic sites to visit, and what local events will be happening so you will have a variety of choices to make. *Yellows* need choices; they do not tolerate being boxed in or having someone else telling them what to do. For *yellows*, the preparation for the trip is as much fun as the trip itself. The challenge is to know everything in advance.

Yellows, although athletic, do not like repetitive physical labor. They would rather hire someone else to perform tasks that are repetitious or mundane. In the workplace, *yellows* are known for delegation of tasks that they feel do not fully utilize their capabilities. This is one of the reasons that *yellows* are most often found in leadership positions. They are systems people. They make lists and review their list many times to ensure that nothing important gets left behind or forgotten. Part of their need to make lists is that their mind is usually so filled with "stuff" that they forget to do what they need to do, such as eating, sleeping, resting, or playing.

At their best, *yellows* are people who can cut through the smokescreens of tradition and focus on the crux of a situation. They have the instinctive insight to be able to see new directions and solutions that will be of the greatest value for all involved. *Yellows* have a keen sense for forecasting and predicting the future, and they are innovative, resourceful thinkers. They can grasp abstract theory easily and convert it into practical applications, and they thrive on complex problems and situations.

Yellows enjoy interaction with people when the conversations are philosophical, intellectual, and non-emotional. They are attracted to people who stimulate their thinking. *Yellows* take criticism very seriously. However, criticism does not intimidate them. If they think they can learn from criticism, they will take it to heart and think about it. On the other hand, if the criticism is viewed as an emotional outburst representing someone else's inability to deal with issues, do not expect *yellows* to sit back and take it. They have an inner sense of rightness and fairness. Do not question their ethics, for they will unleash a strong emotional reaction that is curt, tactless, and often hurtful to others. They can be very aggressive people when their ethics are being challenged. *Yellows* are quick to point out the faults in their attacker's thinking and will openly mount a counterattack. *Yellows* use their intellect as a means of gaining superiority over others.

At their worst, *yellows* are impractical, condescending, overly conceptual, uncompromising, verbose, and nit-picky. They become preoccupied, mentally incapacitated, impatient with others, and irritable. They lose touch with reality and get lost in their heads. Their thinking becomes fuzzy and confused. They get so caught up in trying to rationalize their way of thinking that they lose sight of the objectives. When *yellows* are in this mental state, they tend to intellectualize as a means of not letting others know where they are. They will always take full responsibility for things if appropriate, and if not, they will quickly point out what should be done to correct the situation.

Extroverted Yellows

Extroverted *yellows* are hearty, frank, highly energetic, dynamic, charismatic people. They love to engage people in intellectual banter. They are skilled at persuading others to come over to their way of thinking and support their objectives. They enjoy situations that encourage people to think differently. Extroverted *yellows* are always seeking new challenges. They are the consummate entrepreneurs. If *yellows* are told that something cannot be done but they think it can, they will not only take on the challenge to prove they are right, they will usually exceed expectations. They are masters at fleshing out ideas. They have a natural zest for life and for understanding the complexities of it. They are commandants. They believe it is their place to lead in life and attract people who want to follow their leadership. Their methodology in getting others involved can be likened to the "Tom Sawyer" technique: Make it look easy and so much fun that others cannot possibly resist the temptation to get in and roll up their sleeves to make things happen.

They enjoy public speaking and sharing their thoughts and ideas with people. They understand that in order to be good leaders, they must lead by example. They believe in walking their talk. They know that mixed messages will undermine others' beliefs in them. They are outwardly driven in their thinking, and they need to make things happen. In the game of life, extroverted *yellows* cannot remain on the sidelines. They not only need to be involved in the game, they need to be leading the team.

Introverted Yellows

Introverted *yellows* are the deepest of thinkers. An ideal job for them would be in a "think tank" environment where they would get paid for just thinking. They are constantly creating ideas and concepts and looking for solutions. They have rich imaginations that provide them with endless possibilities to explore. Their thinking process is to consider the possibilities, take action, then reconsider ways to do it better the next time. Introverted *yellows* need the time to think about things, and then think about them some more. They become irritated when pressed to make a decision before they have had the time to fully understand all of the variables. They will probe a problem until they can find the perfect solution. Introverted *yellows* carry on extensive internal mental conversations with themselves. They play out scenario after scenario in their minds and thrive on the complexities of their thoughts. The problem with introverted *yellows* is that most people cannot even comprehend what is going on in their minds. This is because introverted *yellows* do not find it necessary to communicate their thoughts. And, when they do try to explain what they are thinking, it is usually so complicated that others cannot follow them. This adds to their frustration, so they reason, *why try?* It wastes their time and energy.

The faith that introverted *yellows* have in their intuition makes them extremely independent and individualistic. They tend to live by their own intellectual formulas and expect others to fall into line accordingly. They have a real need for autonomy. They are impatient with other people's inability to make decisions, or their emotional outbursts. Introverted *yellows* are cool thinkers under stress, so others will come to them to solve problems when things feel out of control.

For all *yellows*, their greatest gifts are their thinking abilities and their problem-solving skills.

Reflection

*The yellow's world is one of seeking the opportunity
to solve problems and to make things better.
Yellows challenge the status quo because they believe
that everything can be improved upon.
Typically, yellows do not fit in
because they view life so differently.*

*The automobile metaphor would cast the yellow
as the sophisticated, computerized, electronic
and fuel injection systems that enable the vehicle to operate.
Their contributions are recognized,
but no one understands how they work.*

14

The Green Personality

"Green is the fresh emblem of well-founded hopes."
— Mary Webb, author of *The Spring of Joy*

Greens live in a world of hopes, dreams, and emotions where the intangibles of life are the most important. Their rich imaginations thrive when using their creative abilities—their minds work quickly, bouncing from one thought to another. *Greens* think in metaphors and analogies, painting vivid pictures in their minds; *greens* see life from a holistic perspective that allows them to see the complete picture. They love creating ideas and exploring possibilities. Their minds love pondering every alternative; brainstorming with others feeds their need to create and to be around people. Since their preferred mental functioning is totally from the right brain, *greens* are not bound by the limitations and mental barriers that restrict most other types. They focus on what things *could* be rather than what they *are* or are intended to be. *Greens* create novel applications for existing products, services, and operations. When you combine a *green's* ability to see the whole picture with their sensitivity to the feelings and emotions of others, you see that they are capable of creating opportunities and solutions that meet the needs of everyone involved. And, their flair for being different adds an excitement and new twist to the mundane.

Greens have a such clear picture of what is going on that they immediately accept their vision as being real, whether it is or not. The problem *greens* most often face is that they trust and act on their visions and insight so instinctively that they often neglect to find the facts to support the conclusions they have already reached. Worse yet, *greens* can get so emotionally caught up in their visions that they will distort vital details to support them. For example, if you have ever been around *greens* when they are excited and telling you a story, you will notice that they jump around. They get so caught up in their thoughts and trying to tell others how they feel that they forget to finish sentences. This can leave the listener wondering what they are talking about, who are they talking about, and what the point is. It becomes the job of the listener to fill in the blanks and figure out where the story is going. The result is that others have a difficult time staying with a *green's* thinking or taking what they say seriously.

The greatest gift of *greens* is their highly developed intuition. This gift allows them to sense what others are feeling and read between the lines. They rely on their hunches and insight to get a real feel for what is happening. *Greens* are masters at looking for hidden meanings and reading body language. They intuitively interpret motives and nonverbal cues so they can effectively get a sense of the emotional atmosphere of their environment. *Greens*, like *yellows*, are multisensory personalities. The difference is that *greens* instinctively trust their emotions and intuition, where *yellows* do not. *Greens* are the most productive and creative when reacting to their intuition and feelings, rather than to logic and reality. They are more at ease with what *may* be rather than what *is*, almost to the extent of waiting for events to catch up to their visions.

Greens love to learn about themselves. They are open and receptive to new ideas, especially if they can relate to those ideas. They want to know as much as they can about why they act the way they do and how they can make their relationships better. Since they are so unique in their approach to life, they spend a lot of time searching for information that helps them better understand who they are. They seek ways to better learn how to cope in a world that does not necessarily accept their emotionalism. They value inspiration and self-expression above anything else, and follow their inspirations with the energy of a flash flood. It is their enthusiasm that inspires others to want to be around them.

Greens love the experiences that life offers. They are continually looking for new interests and have difficulty staying with things once they lose interest. A *green's* life resembles a succession of projects impulsively chosen, quickly started, often abandoned, and usually incomplete. Greens start out enthusiastically, only to quit upon realizing that structure and repetition are necessary to successfully reach completion or master the necessary skills. A *green* would rather create than do, since they are long on vision and short on action. They look for the fun in life—they enjoy spontaneity and taking things as they happen. They are not great planners; they just believe that everything will happen the way it is supposed to, and trust that whatever comes along will be right.

Greens continually seek to understand what their life's purpose is, the significance of life itself, and also mental, emotional, and spiritual expansion. Their lives are full of events that they see as lessons. Driven to trust and follow their hearts, *greens* are tuned into and sustained by their inner feelings and belief systems. They have an exceptional ability to perceive beauty and wonder in everything around them, both in people and in nature. They view themselves as unique individuals and renaissance people. Greens have an intense need to make their lives count—their lives must have purpose in order for them to feel fulfilled. They believe that they did not come into this life just to take up space, that their life is a self-reflective quest. Always wanting to become their true authentic selves, *greens* can never truly be themselves, since the very act of reaching for self immediately puts it out of reach. This paradox of "one becoming self, if self continues to change" is the burden that *greens* carry throughout their lives. Their endless search for self causes them frustration, guilt, and anxiety. It leaves them believing that their true self is somehow less than it should be.

Greens are driven by idealism and the belief that their purpose in life is to make the world a different and better place. They feel they must influence the quality of life for others. They are the world's greatest cheerleaders, encouraging others to find a better life, and seeking to better understand their true selves. Many motivational and inspirational writers and speakers are *greens*. This personality type is exceptional at using words that inspire, persuade, and motivate. As writers, *greens* understand that the pen is mightier than the sword.

Greens are perpetually curious and always receptive to change. In fact, change is a necessary part of their lives whether it is home, job, mate, lifestyle, or image. Change is their middle name and if their life feels like it is in a rut, then they will change every aspect of it. Unlike other personality types whose natural tendency is to resist change, *greens* welcome the opportunity to experience new things, meet new people, and learn new skills. The risk that *greens* face is that they are so open to anything new or unconventional that they may spend their lives flitting from one thing to another, never staying with one thing long enough to master it. *Greens* have so many talents that it is difficult for them to choose one to focus on. For a *green*, why choose just one thing when you can have it all. It is not uncommon for a *green* to approach midlife wondering why they have not reached their true potential. Part of their frustration results from the fact that they never stay with anything long enough to reap the rewards. *Greens'* lives usually read like a series of short stories with many different scenarios, each one its own adventure.

Of all of the personality types, *greens* are most drawn to and interested in metaphysics, the extrasensory, and the supernatural. It is not unusual to find *greens* involved in some way with the new movements of thinking, for it provides them a forum and setting for their unconventional beliefs; at the same time, it provides them a safe haven where they can pursue their personal quest for spiritual understanding. A new way of thinking allows *greens* to experience things without fear of being viewed as peculiar. It also allows *greens* to develop relationships with people who are of similar inclination. They are attracted to and seek out others who think like they do and who allow them to get in touch with their deepest feelings without being judged.

Greens are warm, sensitive, gentle, emotional people. Their exciting and nurturing energy acts like a magnet when it comes to attracting others. They are masters at subtly engaging the assistance of others by massaging their egos with interesting and sensitive responses. *Greens* openly flatter people and easily express their appreciation. They take great pleasure in pleasing others and making them happy. They tend to develop deep, lasting friendships. When interacting with others, they carefully search for common ground so they can relate. They instinctively create the illusion of providing a safe, emotional, nonjudgmental environment where people can be themselves.

Greens are driven by the need to be liked, and that need is so strong that they are vulnerable to attracting people who are needy or abusive. The potential risk with these relationships is that they drain *greens* emotionally and energetically so they become physically vulnerable. Their need for a relationship drives them so strongly that they feel inadequate without one, so they tend to create relationships that are co-dependent and not healthy for either party. These relationships are usually volatile and may leave both people with deep emotional wounds that never heal. However, it is not uncommon for *greens* to stay in these relationships, because they believe if they just try harder, things might get better. They tend to see relationship failure as their responsibility. *Greens* are so sensitive to the feelings of others that they often take them on as if they were their own, and thus are vulnerable to the emotional manipulation of others who want to dominate them.

Greens are the chameleons of the personality world. These usually gentle, amicable people often surprise others by becoming openly aggressive and hostile when they feel they are being taken advantage of, or are not being appreciated as unique. When a *green* feels put upon or their feelings get hurt, this normally flexible personality becomes *red*. They become rigid, moody, pensive, and argumentative. This behavioral change throws other types off because a *green* will suddenly impose their wishes on others, telling them off or openly seeking revenge for perceived abuses.

Greens, like *oranges*, dislike conflict and will do their best to avoid it. They are happiest and most productive in environments that are conflict free. However, since that is not always possible, *greens* rely on their highly developed gift of intuition to provide them insight into the emotional pulse of their environment. Their intuitive sense acts like a radar system, alerting them to any potential for conflict. When *greens* are in a conflict situation, they tend to believe that to differ with a person would mean to reject them personally, and because they cannot face the possibility of being rejected, they will keep quiet and withdraw. *Greens* will also steer clear of conversations that are heavy or have the potential for conflict. Instead, they prefer to involve themselves in discussions that are self-directed or full of intrigue. *Greens* love romance, melodrama, and involvement in interactions that feed their imagination.

Greens are natural champions of the downtrodden, the environment, and human rights. They base their judgments subjectively on human, aesthetic, and civil values. Their interest in their fellow human beings and the environment is genuine. As the humanitarians of the world, they will become relentless when fighting for deeply held beliefs. They will commit whatever it takes to redress social injustice: time, money, or energy. Their dedication to a particular cause is directly tied to the pull it has on their heartstrings.

Extroverted Greens

An extroverted *green's* motto is "Ready-fire-aim." These *greens* are more interested in jumping right in and getting started than they are in figuring out what needs to be done and in what sequence. Consequently, they spend a lot of time having to redo. They rely on their abilities to intuitively know what needs to be done rather than preparing in advance. Extroverted *greens* are high-spirited and have a zest for life that is a combination of enthusiasm, effervescence, and social gregariousness. Their philosophy is to maximize life's options. For these *greens*, life is full of endless possibilities and alternatives and a host of interpersonal encounters just waiting to happen. The problem is that they get so caught up in their current projects or interests that they think of little else.

When the chips are down, you can always count on a *green* to come through with something positive to say that will inspire. They are experts at rallying the troops together by calling on their sense of creativity, perseverance, and humor. They are witty and clever and tell jokes and stories to lighten things up. They always look for the rainbow even in the darkest of times. They have the capacity to motivate and make others feel that they can accomplish anything, and they tend to take on a fearless persona. They love to be the center of attention and lead others by their enthusiasm.

Extroverted *greens* tend to think out loud and need input and direction. They will openly seek emotional counsel from people when trying to make a decision. Their pattern is such that they will ask someone for their opinion and then will make their decision based on what that person said. The problem begins when they go to another person and ask them for their input and once again change their mind. This changing of one's mind with every person they talk to sends mixed signals. It confuses others and can become a source of frustration to those who work or live with them. Before too long, people start to ask themselves why they should take the time to provide feedback. They know the *green* is just going to change their mind depending on what input has just been received.

Introverted Greens

Introverted *greens* present quite the opposite persona from their extroverted counterparts. They are calm, quiet, reserved, and even shy. They do not like to be the center of attention. In fact, they are more interested in hearing about others than talking about themselves. Although they may demonstrate a cool reserve, they are loving, warm people. They have a capacity for a depth of caring that is not generally found in the other types. However, introverted *greens* are very particular about whom they share their feelings with. They must feel very safe and secure with a person before they will open up.

Unlike extroverted *greens*, introverted *greens* find self-expression difficult. Being reflective, contemplative, meditative, and inwardly focused people, they derive pleasure from interacting with their own active imaginations. Good listeners and sympathetic observers, they love to watch and listen to people and enjoy internalizing what they perceive. Once they get to know you and determine you are someone they like, they are open and enthusiastic.

For these *greens*, a harmonious environment is very important to their emotional well-being. If subjected to hostile, conflict-ridden environments, they internalize their feelings so deeply that they withdraw and find it difficult to deal with the world. Introverted *greens* find that being reclusive is very appealing. For them, life is often so emotionally brutal that they withdraw into their own world just to survive.

🦋

Reflection
The green's world is filled with optimism, dreams, and fantasies. Their role is to create and to learn. Greens are involved in life and respond to it with emotion and enthusiasm.

In the automobile, the green would be the rich leather seats, the eight-speaker sound system, and the convertible top—the fun stuff.

🦋 🦋 🦋

15

The Role of Personality in Illness

"Every situation properly perceived becomes the opportunity to heal."
— A Course in Miracles

Roxanne was a *green* personality type. She came to see me because she was unable to get pregnant and was concerned, at age 38, that time was running out. She told me that ever since she was a child, she had dreamed of having her own family. At age 32, she finally met Mr. Right. For six years, they had been trying to start their family, to no avail. She had seen many doctors and was told there was nothing physically wrong that would prevent her from having children. This confused and dismayed her. It created a tremendous amount of stress in her relationship and in herself. The reason that she came to me was to see if perhaps I could provide some insight into what could be preventing her from getting pregnant. She was curious to know if there were any blockages energetically, emotionally, or psychologically that were preventing conception. Roxanne's desire to have a child had turned into an obsession. She was frustrated and disappointed with herself. In her words, "I am a mess. My body is a mess and my life is a mess."

It did not take me long to identify stress as one of the primary contributors to her problem—the stress of trying to function as someone other than who she really was. She was a *green* personality trying to live her life as a *red* most of the time. If you go back and read the descriptions of the *green* and *red* personalities, you too will see that the way each of these types thinks and approaches life is very different.

Roxanne was vice president of marketing for a large corporation. Her job responsibilities were very demanding and required her to travel frequently. While she liked parts of her job and the opportunity to meet new people and to experience new things, the pace was draining energetically, emotionally, mentally, and physically. Roxanne took the job thinking that it would be creative and allow her to implement many of her ideas, but she found that there was no time for creativity. Responsible for managing details and coordinating the efforts of 16 people, her work required that she deal with deadlines and maintain a very disciplined time schedule. She was always tired, a point that her boss brought to her attention regularly. She was always behind and could never seem to fit everything in. When she finally got home, there never seemed to be time to relax and unwind. Always playing catch-up, she was spreading herself thin—frequently to the point of physical exhaustion.

The stress that was created from her having to function as a different personality color for a prolonged period of time was taking its toll on her health, her relationship, and her life. She felt that her life was difficult and had lost its joy. *Greens* need to have fun and feel free. She was feeling trapped and did not know how to get out of it. She thought if she just tried harder and managed her time better, she could manage it.

As a *green*, Roxanne's weak site was her chest and upper neck area. She suffered regularly from shoulder and neck muscle tension, hyperthyroidism, high blood pressure, frequent coughing, and a shortness of breath. Trying to live her life as a *red* personality whose weak site is the pelvic area, she had developed many typical *red* symptoms. Her hormones were out of balance, and there was a large energy protrusion in her pelvic area, specifically her uterus. What I found was that the hardness that she felt in life had manifested itself into a fibroid cyst in the uterus. There were indicators of endometriosis and a lesion on the right ovary; when I asked if her doctor had discussed these problems with her, she said no. I suggested she go back to her doctor and confirm my findings. Because Roxanne kept telling herself that she was a mess and both her thoughts and emotions supported that belief, she was actually creating that mess inside of her—her emotions were on a roller coaster, her thinking was confused, and her body was chemically out of balance. While all of these factors were significant enough to contribute to her inability to become pregnant, from my perspective the primary factor was that she had been functioning for so long as someone other than whom she really was. The price she was paying was affecting her health.

The first thing I suggested was that she learn more about who she really was. If she better understood herself, her core personality color, and its strengths and weaknesses, then she could learn how to function as another color without it taking so much out of her. I suggested that she begin to embrace the *green* that she was. Not only would she be more productive, but she would also get back her sense of joy and satisfaction from life. Next, I suggested that she find out if the travel could be reduced. While *greens* love new experiences and the change that travel offers, it is very difficult for them. For *greens*, their home is their sanctuary and the place they go to cocoon and put themselves back together. Without the anchor of home, they get off center. Another suggestion was that she and her husband spend more time together to reestablish the bonds that brought them together in the first place. My final suggestion was that she lighten up on herself, quit trying so hard, and stop being so negative. I encouraged her to listen to her self-talk and specifically stop telling herself that everything was a mess. As long as she kept doing so, she would continue to be a mess. Her session strongly validated the premise that our personality and the impact it has on our lives plays a significant role in why we become ill.

I do not always get feedback from my sessions; however, in this case, Roxanne shared that she had gone home and announced to her husband that she was a *green* personality and needed to start living like one again. She explained what a *green* was, and he told her that was who he fell in love with, and he had been concerned because she had changed so much. They talked about her job. While he knew how much she liked it, he was very supportive of less travel. He told her that he was lonely and missed spending time with his best friend. They both made the decision that if the travel could not be reduced, she would seek another position. As it turned out, a job change was not necessary because her boss had already planned to talk to her about redefining her job responsibilities and eliminating most of her traveling.

Those changes would also require her to be more creative. Roxanne went back to her doctor and had her listen to the part of the audiocassette from her reading concerning the fibroid cyst and endometriosis. The doctor confirmed both and also found the lesion on the right ovary. Steps were taken to correct the problems.

Roxanne's mother sat in front of me ten months after my session with Roxanne. She told me that Roxanne is a completely different person, back to her old self, and three months pregnant. While not all stories have happy endings, the case of Roxanne was different because she was willing to do whatever was necessary to get what she wanted. Her story shows that if we are willing to accept who we are and change what is preventing us from fulfilling our desires, anything is possible.

Illness—an Information Source

Illness is our body's way of telling us that something is not working right. It acts as a feedback system alerting us that there is a breakdown in the internal communication network between the body, mind, and spirit. Illness has a purpose—it creates an awareness that the natural rhythmic patterns of the body have been interrupted by some imbalance or malfunction. These imbalances or malfunctions, whether energetic or chemical in nature, inhibit the body's ability to function properly. When illness occurs, we must focus on and listen to what it is telling us so we can restore it back to its proper functioning.

Illness has many meanings, some more obvious than others. When illness occurs in the physical body, it is easy to interpret what it is trying to tell us because of the physical symptoms it creates. Physical symptoms immediately get the attention of the mind and tell it what the body needs. For instance, maybe it needs more sleep, a change in diet, a change in lifestyle, less stress, or more exercise. How do we interpret what that illness is trying to tell us at a deeper level—say, at the level of our energy system? Illness created at this level is our spirit's way of telling us that we have forgotten to recognize the important role it plays in our overall state of health and well-being. It reminds us that the spiritual self is just as important as the physical self. And, if we are to remain healthy and keep the physical body functioning properly, it too needs to be fed, nurtured, and exercised. We cannot neglect our spirit without creating an imbalance or malfunction in all other aspects of who we are: mental, emotional, or physical.

Illness created at the mental level is telling us that we need to change our thoughts, perceptions, and beliefs. Many of the inabilities and hidden blocks associated with illness lie more in our beliefs than in our bodies. Listen to your self-talk and learn to "eavesdrop" on your thoughts. For example, if you are always saying, "I'm confused," it will create confusion in the mind and a sense of not being in control of your life.

"This job is killing me" weakens the immune system. "That person is a real pain in the neck" literally can create a pain in the neck. Oh, and how about, "You make me sick." That one really gets us and in fact creates illness throughout the entire body. If your thoughts are negative and self-critical, then they can trigger strong emotional reactions that can manifest what you are thinking. If your thoughts do not promote your feeling good about yourself, then you will not feel good, period.

At an emotional level, illness is telling us how our thoughts are affecting us. Emotions are judgments we create that support our thinking and beliefs. They tell the truth about where we are in life. What I have found in my work with the energy system is that the majority of the illnesses are created within the emotional layer of energy. I have learned that it is the type of emotions people create and how they deal with their emotions that has the most significant impact on their health. When we create emotions that cause a negative reaction such as anger, hatred, hostility, resentment, guilt, or frustration, we create a chemical toxicity in the body that weakens it and increases the potential for illness and infection. Emotions that we do not deal with end up leaving deep hurts and wounds that we often carry throughout our entire lives. When we give power to our emotional hurts, we give away our personal power. I have also learned that while we all share many of the same fears, insecurities, anxieties, and emotional reactions, each of the four different personality types tends to have very specific issues that affect specific areas of the body.

New scientific evidence in the fields of behavioral and energy medicine is supporting the premise that the real cause of illness lies in our thoughts and emotions, and those two factors affect the endocrine system, the chemistry of the body, and the immune system. What researchers are learning about illness is that people who consistently become ill show very specific patterns, including:

1. Viewing life from a negative perspective
2. Inability to deal with their emotions and having unresolved emotional issues that consume their thoughts
3. Unwillingness to change patterns of behavior that are negative and self-destructive
4. Inability to give and receive love
5. Lacking a sense of humor to help relieve the seriousness of life
6. A tendency to deny themselves the things that would improve their quality of life
7. Feeling powerless to make their own choices
8. Inability to remain flexible so they can flow with life's challenges
9. Seeing their life as pointless and having no meaning or purpose
10. Not attending to the needs of their physical body
11. Unwillingness to manage stress

Illness robs us of energy and of life itself. It distorts the messages being sent between the mind and body, and throws every part of us out of sync. Illness involves the whole person, not just specific sites within the body where symptoms are surfacing. When you look at illness and what causes it, look at it from all aspects of your life. Consider your lifestyle, your relationships with others, your relationship with yourself, what creates stress in your life, your fears, your personality type, and the habits you create as a result of your personality type. Dr. Bernie Siegel, author and inspirational speaker, reminds us that there are no incurable illnesses, only incurable people.

Personality and Illness

There is a direct correlation between the genetic aspect of our personality and illness. That aspect directs the way our mind communicates with our physical body and the habits we create. When it comes to our health, how we think and react directly affects the balance and well-being of our body. Since personality is something that is instinctive, we tend to take it for granted. We forget to pay attention to the habits and the comfort zones we create as a result of it. While these habits and comfort zones help us function effectively in one aspect of our life, they may in fact inhibit and even sabotage another aspect of our life, such as our health.

Let me show you what I mean. Personalities who are *reds* and *oranges* are well equipped to deal with reality and basic survival needs because of their personality strengths and their approach to life. Yet, in order to help themselves cope, they tend to create habits such as smoking, drinking, and taking medications to help them relax. These personalities are usually so busy living, working, and taking care of the basic human needs of others that they forget to take time to care for themselves. They are so intense in their focus that they tend to stay tense for longer periods of time, and consequently suffer from lower back pain, and aches and pains in the muscles and joints. When I ask them about their health habits, it is not uncommon to hear them say that they are too busy to find the time to put something together on a routine basis. When I ask them about getting sick, I have had many *reds* and *oranges* tell me that they do not have time to get sick, so their bodies had better cooperate and learn how to take care of themselves.

Now, let's look at each one of the personality colors and the effect they may have on health. As we cover each of the four colors, I will identify some of the most common emotional and psychological issues that each color struggles with; where their weak sites are in the body; which glands, organs and major systems of the body are affected; and list some of the potential types of illness each personality has a predisposition for developing.

Before we begin the process of self-exploration, let me first define what I mean by "weak site." In the energy system, the weak site is where the root cause of illness originates. The energetic information contained within the weak site identifies if the illness was created within the emotional or mental layer of energy. It points out the severity of the chemical change in the body and which other parts of the body will be affected.

In the physical body, the weak site is the most vulnerable part of the body that has the greatest susceptibility to imbalance, illness, and malfunction. It is where most symptoms of illness will first surface. Take a moment and think about your health and which areas in your body are the source of the greatest problems. Now, go back and look at your childhood health issues. You will probably find that the majority of your illnesses always tended to be in one area of your body. Perhaps you suffered more from respiratory problems or digestive problems or structural and skeletal problems or problems with elimination. Each one of these health issues is directly connected to specific weak sites in the body.

With respect to personality, the weak site contains information that identifies how a person mentally functions and relates to their external world. It reveals what kinds of emotional and psychological issues the person consistently struggles with. It identifies the predictable behavioral patterns that determine the person's approach to life and how they deal with the challenges that life offers them.

Behavioral Patterns and Weak Site of the Red Personality

Reds work too hard and are continually pushing themselves, often to the point of physical exhaustion. They are prime candidates for health issues because of the way they deal with stress. They are excitable personalities who anger easily, and they become vocal and physically aggressive when feeling threatened. Their eating habits are such that it is not uncommon for them to miss meals, eat only one meal a day, or grab something quick just to satisfy their hunger. They tend to have difficulty relaxing or getting a good night's sleep. When they're tired, *reds* become emotionally overwhelmed, sometimes to the point of being distraught. In this mental state they cannot think clearly or cope with anything. They become repetitious in what they say, somehow thinking that repetition will help them achieve clarity of thought. They will create multiple problems so they can avoid having to deal with real issues. Their insecurities arise when they feel "unsafe" in their environment. *Reds* tend to display obsessive-compulsive behavioral patterns, especially when feeling out of control. Some of the emotional and psychological anxieties and insecurities that *reds* display are:

1. Fear of not being able to provide basic human necessities
2. Fear of being emotionally vulnerable
3. Fear of poverty
4. Fear of being powerless
5. Paranoia around personal safety and security
6. Fear of loss of personal possessions and financial assets
7. Fear of other people taking advantage of them financially
8. Fear of personal intimacy
9. Anxieties that they cannot make things happen the way they need them to in order to feel some measure of success

10. Frustration around not being able to control people and their environment
11. Fear of being out of control
12. Feeling sorry for self
13. Avoidance of emotional needs and deep feelings
14. Exaggerating the truth in order to make others think they are in control or important
15. Sexual anxieties

Weak site: A *red's* weak site is in the pelvic area, legs, feet, and entire spinal column. The systems affected are the immune system, digestive system, and circulatory system. The glands and organs affected are the reproductive organs, adrenals, and spleen.

Potential health issues: Hypertension, heart disease, stroke, hyperthyroidism, chronic lower back pain, sciatica, bowel and rectal disorders, pelvic hip and joint disorders, tumor and cancer of pelvic area, pelvic inflammatory diseases, prostate cancer, leg cramps, circulation problems in legs and feet, phlebitis, varicose veins, ulcers, anxiety attacks, chronic stress syndrome, alcohol abuse, indigestion, diarrhea, impotency, urinary infections, osteoarthritis, blood ailments, and insomnia.

Behavioral Patterns and Weak Site of the Orange Personality

Oranges are worriers. They continually live with a low level of anxiety about life. They tend to take on too much and let other people's problems become their own. They strive too hard to fulfill the needs of others. They struggle with the conflict between the responsibilities of family and work. *Oranges* need familiarity and security and become anxious when either are in jeopardy. When stressed, they become erratic and suffer from emotional outbursts and deep states of depression. Their outlook on life becomes negative, and life itself becomes hard. When depressed, they use food as a means of emotional comfort, and they tend to struggle with weight issues. This personality type has a predisposition toward addictions: alcohol, substance abuse, gambling, and compulsive spending. They are passive-aggressive in their behavior and have a tendency to hold in their emotions until they reach a boiling point; then they let loose and immediately feel guilty for doing so. Some of the emotional and psychological anxieties and insecurities displayed by *oranges* are:

1. Fear of abandonment
2. Fear of being unsupported by others; of being alone
3. Anxieties around never having enough
4. Fear of being taken advantage of, being manipulated and controlled
5. Feelings of guilt and resentment toward others when not appreciated
6. Fear of loss of job or family
7. Feelings of being victimized by one's circumstances, sexual preferences, or ethnic origin
8. Inability to take responsibility for their lives
9. Feeling powerless to make their own choices
10. Denying themselves what they need to maintain their quality of life
11. Fear of not being able to take care of themselves financially
12. Frustrations around sexuality and sexual performance
13. Feelings of resentment over others having control over them
14. Fear of the unknown
15. Feelings of guilt around not being an adequate partner in their relationship

Weak site: An *orange's* weak site is the lower abdomen and lower back (specifically lumbar and sacral spinal area). The areas affected are the reproductive, respiratory, circulatory, and muscle systems. The glands and organs affected are the pancreas, reproductive organs (ovaries and testes), thyroid, small and large intestine, bladder, and kidneys.

Potential health issues: Men: prostate, hormone imbalance, impotency, testicular cancer. Women: menstrual difficulties, vaginitis, fibroid cysts and tumors in uterus, ovarian cysts, endometriosis, hormone imbalances, and breast, cervical, uterine, and ovarian cancer. Fibromyalgia, rheumatoid arthritis, diabetes, manic depression, candidiasis, chronic mid- and lower-back pain, disk problems (ruptured or slipped disks), chronic fatigue syndrome, pancreatitis, pancreatic cancer, kidney disease, urinary infections, kidney stones, mental exhaustion, and constipation.

Behavioral Patterns and Weak Site of the Yellow Personality

Yellows are perfectionists; they expect perfection from themselves and everyone else. They constantly push themselves by escalating their personal standards of excellence. They are extremely critical and judgmental of themselves and others. They have a deep inner fear of failure. They have issues around trust and are naturally suspicious of people and what their real motives are. Their work is their life, so they tend to become singularly focused, leaving little time for relaxation or for other people. Their frustration is around people who are illogical and who display emotional outbursts. They are resentful of people pushing them to make decisions before they are ready. When stressed, *yellows* get nit-picky and argumentative. They become indignant when accused of doing something that is not honest or ethical; their behavior instantly changes and they become aggressive and show open hostility. Their analytical nature creates constant conflict between what their head thinks and their heart feels. When caught in this thinking dilemma, they experience despair, confusion, and self-doubt; they become immobilized. They lose their confidence and withdraw deeper into themselves, which leaves others wondering what is wrong. *Yellows* do not share their emotions, so others do not know how to help them. They become antisocial. The truth is that when in this state of mind, *yellows* do not want help. They need to work things out themselves. Some of the emotional and psychological anxieties and insecurities displayed by *yellows* are:

1. Fear of rejection and criticism
2. Fear of intimidation
3. Fear of failure
4. Frustration resulting from being pushed by others and told what to do
5. Worrying about having to be accountable to others
6. Anger and resentment resulting from having their integrity questioned
7. Frustration over relationships that are emotionally complex
8. Feeling entrapped in a needy relationship
9. Fear of accepting responsibility for themselves and their commitments
10. Fear of loss of independence and autonomy
11. Resentment over having to take responsibility for others who are incapable of taking care of themselves
12. Self-deception
13. Lack of faith in themselves
14. Fear of looking stupid or incompetent
15. Inability to express and show emotions

Weak site: A *yellow's* weak site is the solar plexus and midback (specifically the thoracic section of the spine). The areas affected are the digestive, immune, central nervous, and skeletal systems. The glands and organs affected are the pituitary and adrenal glands, skin, stomach, liver, gall bladder, spleen, and lower esophagus.

Potential health issues: Chronic digestive disorders, gastritis, stomach cancer, liver disorders, liver cancer, gallstones, ulcers, spastic colon, colitis, autoimmune diseases, lupus, hiatal hernia, chronic stress syndrome, multiple sclerosis, ALS (Lou Gehrig's disease), skin disorders, allergies, herpes simplex virus, herpes zoster virus, arthritis, tendinitis, anemia, mononucleosis, headaches, paralysis, and adrenal dysfunction.

Behavioral Patterns and Weak Site of the Green Personality

Greens suppress their feelings. They will avoid conflict even at their own expense. They blame themselves and continually feel guilty for everything that happens. They accept responsibility for others' faults and see those faults as their own. They are afraid to say no for fear of hurting someone's feelings. They struggle with the feeling that they are not worthy of being loved. How they feel about themselves is directly tied to what is happening in their relationships. For them, life without love is frightening. They tend to involve themselves in relationships that are emotionally needy, abusive, or not fulfilling. Rejection is devastating emotionally. They wear their hearts on their sleeves for all to see and take advantage of. They can get so caught up in their emotionalism that they lose all objectivity in coping with the real world. They struggle with the inner turmoil of trying to find themselves and how they fit into this world. They tend to feel sorry for themselves and wallow in self-condemnation. When neglected, they become bitter, insensitive, and even cruel. They project dependent-submissive behavioral patterns toward others. Some of the emotional and psychological anxieties and insecurities displayed by greens are:

1. Fear that others will use their vulnerabilities against them
2. Frustration with respect to being responsible for the feelings of others
3. Fear of not being loved
4. Confusion around love and what it means
5. Fickleness toward others
6. Jealousy
7. Resentment from holding on to past hurts and emotional abusiveness
8. Depression associated with lack of self-love
9. Harboring negative feelings toward others
10. Self-destructive behavior that perpetuates feelings of inadequacy

11. Fear of being alone
12. Feelings used as an escape or to deny responsibility for their actions
13. Creating co-dependent relationships
14. Tending to stay in relationships that are personally destructive
15. Frustration over the inability to step up to issues and make decisions

Weak site: A *green's* weak site is the chest, shoulders, upper back (cervical spinal area), and neck. The areas affected are the circulatory, respiratory, immune, cerebrospinal, and muscle systems. The glands and organs affected are the thyroid, thymus, pituitary, pineal, lungs, heart, and pancreas.

Potential health issues: Upper neck and muscle tension, migraine headaches, diabetes, thyroid disorders, hypo/hyperglycemia, breast cancer, heart disease, mitral valve prolapse, asthma, chronic respiratory disorder, depression, eating disorders (anorexia and bulimia), hormone imbalances, tinnitus, epilepsy, muscular dystrophy, attention deficit disorder, neurological disorders, bone cancer, allergies, laryngitis, and nervous disorders.

Healing Happens When We Help It

While research is still in the discovery stages with respect to understanding how thoughts and emotions actually relate to the brain's release of chemicals, what has been discovered is that the personality has a direct impact on the creation of thoughts, emotional reactions, and the health of the body. What we now know is that our state of mind directly affects the chemistry of the body in such a way that we are either becoming ill or overcoming illness every moment of our lives. The human body is an extraordinary mechanism that has an astonishing and irrepressible need to stay healthy. It is constantly repairing, renewing, and regenerating itself. Our job is to help it succeed. We can do this by better understanding ourselves, changing our habits, altering our thinking, making path corrections, and eliminating from our lives what is preventing us from staying healthy.

❦

Reflection

Personality ties behavioral and emotional responses to the body.
The body responds by creating weak sites predictable by personality color.

Prepared with the knowledge and understanding of our personality colors,
we have an increased awareness of the vulnerability of our state of wellness.

❦   ❦   ❦

PART IV

Connecting the Physical to the Spiritual

16

Chakras—the Spiritual Energy Centers of the Body

"A thousand colors but the Light is one."
— Lao Tzu

C hakras, meaning "spinning wheels of light," are the spiritual energy centers of the human body, and were first mentioned in ancient Sanskrit texts. These spinning wheels of light are responsible for the creation and absorption of energy and form a glow of light around people, which is called the *aura*. The ancient texts stated that the chakras were conduits of electromagnetic energy through which the inner spiritual self could express itself physically. The writings tell of seven chakras of light found within the human body, each of which has their own vibrational frequency, which is seen as a different color of light. It is through the light and colors of the chakras that mystics, metaphysicians, and intuitives determine where imbalance, malfunction, and illness is occurring in the body.

Over the past 15 years, great strides have been made in validating the existence of chakras and learning more about them. What has been discovered is that each chakra transmits a distinct frequency, and by listening to the differences in frequencies, it is possible to map out specifically where in the body each one of the chakras is located. What was confirmed is that there are seven chakras within the structure of the human body—the first chakra being at the base of the spine, the second in the lower abdomen, the third in the solar plexus, the fourth in the upper chest, the fifth in the throat, the sixth at the center of the forehead, and the seventh at the crown of the head. The structure of each chakra looks like a flattened bell-shaped funnel. These funnels create vortices of spiraling energy that are in a constant state of movement. At their narrowest point, the funnels are less than one-eighth of an inch in diameter and actually touch the surface of the human body. This contact of energy is what is released from the body and seen as the aura.

The chakras as a collective unit form a system that generates the electromagnetic field of energy found in the human aura. The chakras serve as conduits of energy and electrochemical information that can be utilized by the human body to tell it how to maintain balance. The chakra system's primary function is to receive, translate, and transmit the energetic information it gathers and relay that information, both to the brain for processing, and to specific sites within the body. When studying the relationship between the chakra system and the physical body, one finds a wonderful natural intelligence that is evident in the way they interface to create the intricate communication network found in the human energy system. When you think of the chakra system, think of it as the organizing force that orchestrates the dialogue between the body, mind, and spirit. The information it contains expresses itself in the four energy layers: spiritual, emotional, mental, and physical.

Each chakra rotates at a specific speed and creates its own "fingerprint" frequency that synchronizes with the corresponding frequency of one of the seven endocrine glands found in the human body. Each chakra is a critical regulator for the balance and flow of energy. The amount of energy that each chakra produces, releases, and absorbs is affected by internal and external factors. When chakras are open to receiving and transmitting information, they rotate in a spiraling clockwise motion. If any chakra becomes energetically overstimulated and, as a result, depleted, then it reverses its flow, shuts down its receptivity, and ceases transmitting information. This change in flow interrupts the natural rhythmic flow of energy and creates energetic congestion and blockage, both of which lead to imbalance and malfunction in the physical body.

While each chakra has its own frequency and appears to function independently from the others, they are in fact interdependent in maintaining the health of the physical body. Any change in one affects its immediate neighbors and consequently all the other chakras. For example, if the third chakra (solar plexus) decreases its output of energy flow because of stress it created in the physical body when over-stimulated, then the fourth chakra (heart) or the second chakra (lower abdomen) must compensate for the loss of energy by increasing their output. This adjustment of energy is another of the functions of the chakra system and usually takes place without any impact on the physical body. When the chakra system is balanced, then all chakras work in unison and each evenly absorbs and distributes energy. In an unhealthy chakra system, the lines of communication break down, and energy blockages occur. The result is that all chakras lose their vitality, and the physical body becomes ill. The chakra system is no different than any other system within the physical body. It must maintain balance in order to function properly.

Each chakra and the cellular structure surrounding it has the capacity to store information. Just as the immune system remembers viral invaders, the chakras remember physiological, psychological, and emotional changes. Physiological changes encompass the metabolic, chemical, cellular (DNA), hormonal, and growth areas. Emotional and psychological changes include habitual patterns of behavior, thoughts, and emotional reactions. Each chakra is specialized in how it decodes information and uses it. This ability to remember allows the chakras to energetically mirror any changes happening in the physical body. Each chakra is always choosing, formatting, analyzing, and monitoring the information it is receiving. After each chakra has finished processing the data it receives, it transmits that information to the other chakras. It is then up to all the chakras to interpret and use the information in such a way that balance will be maintained.

The Seven Major Chakras

Each of the seven chakras has a specific responsibility with respect to how its energy communicates with the physical body. The first chakra, located at the base of the spine, is responsible for energizing and strengthening the entire body. The second controls and energizes the sexual organs and the lower digestive system. The third activates the adrenal glands and energizes the entire digestive tract. The fourth stimulates the circulatory system and energizes the heart and thymus gland. The fifth regulates the thyroid gland and energizes throat activity. The sixth is responsible for the communication linkage between the pituitary gland and the other endocrine glands of the body. The seventh chakra stimulates the activities of the brain and energizes the pineal gland, which in ancient times was considered the seat of the soul.

The lower three chakras energetically respond to issues that pertain to physical survival and interaction with others. The fourth chakra is the fulcrum point through which we find balance and stability between our physical self and spiritual self. The fifth is our self-expression chakra. It allows us to tell others who we are. The sixth and seventh are our spiritual chakras—they respond energetically to our need for a deeper understanding of self.

The different vibrational frequencies of the seven chakras radiate different colors. The first chakra is *red*, which excites and stimulates. The second is *orange*, which stimulates creativity, vitality, and sexual expression. The third chakra's color is *yellow*, a warm color that stimulates the linear thinking activity of the mind and encourages one to get in touch with their personal power. The fourth is *green*, a healing color that represents the need to get back in balance. The fifth is *blue*, an excellent color for calming the body and encouraging relaxation. The sixth is *indigo*, which neutralizes the effects of the yellow color, relaxing the mind so that we can integrate intuition into our processing of information. This activates whole brain thinking. The seventh chakra is *violet*, a spiritual color that represents enlightenment, and the perfect balance between the physical and the spiritual. This color stimulates the desire to explore the connection between ourselves and the divine.

Each of the seven chakras (because of their ability to retain information) reacts to specific psychological and emotional patterns of behavior, which comprise a lifetime of experiences, beliefs, and attitudes. If we explore the energetic responses of each chakra, we would find that those responses are just as predictable as the patterns of behavior we find in the different personality types.

The First Chakra—the Power Center for Control of the Physical World

The first chakra energetically responds to issues dealing with our physical reality. It is our grounding chakra, and its energy drives behavior that enables us to manifest our desires. It relies on the five senses in order to determine the proper energetic response. The behavior associated with this chakra is the need for safety and personal survival. The activity of this chakra deals with matters relating to the material world, a person's sense of success, and the physical body. This chakra dominates traditional societal mores, and drives behavior that allows us to conform to and fit into society—it is our belong-and-serve chakra. It is also the chakra whose energy responds to the thoughts and emotions that we have regarding the relationship we have with our family. It is our sexual pleasure chakra and the procreation center of the body. This chakra responds to sensory gratification and the need for physical contact.

The Second Chakra—the Power Center for Emotional Control of Other People

The second chakra is what I call the human emotion chakra. It is the power center of emotions, and influences how we use them to gain control over ourselves and others. It is where we house emotional patterns that provide behavioral guidelines that tell us how to react to situations based on what we have learned. It encompasses those societal patterns of behavior that help us better fit into society, which we learned as children. The emotional patterns of this chakra are formed based on expectations, and are judgmental in nature. Behavior is driven by do and don't, good and bad, right or wrong, and should or should not. Negative patterns of behavior displayed through this chakra are limiting—they inhibit positive feelings of self-worth, and create feelings of emotional dependency. The energy of the second chakra is also social in nature. It drives our need to seek relationships with others, and its energy encourages us to put the emotional needs of others before our own. This chakra creates the desires that the first chakra works to bring to fruition—desires such as financial abundance, the accumulation of material objects, and emotional security. The energy of this chakra is also related to our sexuality and the desire for procreation.

The Third Chakra—the Power Center for Control of Self

The third chakra is our mental chakra. Its energy is associated with both intuitive and linear information processing. As the thinker part of who we are, it is our common sense chakra and draws upon its stored memory to direct the choices we make. I refer to this chakra as our mainframe computer. Unlike the other chakras, which only store information pertaining specifically to them, the third chakra stores all thoughts, experiences, memories, habits, and perceptions. Every bit of information received and transmitted throughout the chakra system first flows through the third chakra for analysis. It is responsible for providing first-impression feedback, which it expresses by sending us gut feelings. The third chakra maintains balance between our thoughts and emotions, and it relies on the second chakra to provide the emotional feedback. This chakra, like the first, responds to issues dealing with physical reality. The behavior associated with this chakra is that of solving problems and of being in control. The energy from this chakra provides us with a sense of personal power. It supports our beliefs about ourselves, whether those beliefs are positive or negative. When positively charged, its energy empowers us and gives us a feeling of having control over our own destiny. The positive behavior associated with this chakra is self-confidence, self-trust, self-respect, and self-development.

The Fourth Chakra—the Power Center for Self-Love and Self-Esteem

This is our main life-support chakra, both physically and emotionally. The feelings that we house in the heart chakra are those of self-love and self-esteem—not the self-esteem that we seek through the second chakra where others are responsible for how we feel about ourselves, but that which we create by going inside and looking at our personal successes. This chakra is responsible for balancing the physical self with the spiritual self. Its energy acts as a conduit through which the spiritual emotions (sixth chakra) can flow to the human emotions (second chakra). This chakra is responsible for the creation of the unconditional love we display toward others and ourselves. It expresses its behavior through the emotions of love, compassion, forgiveness, understanding, and sensitivity; its energy is that of healing. The behavior displayed by the fourth chakra is one of a personal quest—finding meaning for one's existence, having a sense of purpose, and understanding one's self better.

The Fifth Chakra—the Power Center for Self-Expression

The fifth chakra's energy encourages us to find our voice, and express to others what we want and need. The development of this chakra is directly tied to the emotional reactions found within the second chakra. If as a child you were discouraged from speaking out or even punished for doing so, then as an adult, speaking up for yourself may not be a comfortable thing to do. The inability to speak up for oneself sends the message to others that one is submissive and easily controlled. If people want to change how others see them, then they will have to learn to express themselves and become accountable for the words they use. The energy of this chakra actively interacts with all seven chakras, for it is this chakra that all thoughts and emotions will flow through to be communicated to others. The behavior associated with this chakra encourages asking questions and having internal conversations with the self. It is the speaker of truth and of our divine will.

The Sixth Chakra—the Power Center for Inner Wisdom

The sixth chakra expresses itself through the use of creativity and imagination. It is the center of our intuition and is the portal of energy through which we pass when we want to learn more about our inner self and explore our higher states of consciousness. The exploration of self through this chakra taps into our deepest subconscious psyche, which holds within it the spiritual truths that our conscious mind cannot surface, remember, or even comprehend. The energy associated with the sixth chakra integrates spiritual perception, and the use of the sixth sense, with our logical thinking. As the home for our spiritual emotions—optimism, joy, and love—it adds a different perspective to the issues we are dealing with in our physical reality. Its behavior expresses itself through our humor and artistic abilities, and our insight. The sixth chakra does not relate to the emotions of the second chakra, which are judgmental and restrictive. Thus, these emotions flow through the fourth chakra so they can be translated energetically into something that the second chakra emotions can deal with. The spiritual emotions are always encouraging us to release the emotional patterns of the second chakra that bind us to self-destructive habits. The emotions found in the sixth chakra have no judgments attached to them; instead, they see events in life as opportunities to grow and cannot relate to limitations.

The Seventh Chakra—the Power Center for Connecting the Self with the Divine

The seventh chakra's energy connects us with what we call God and our higher self. It is the gateway that we must go through if we are to access the highest spiritual influences within each of us. Its energy balances our spiritual self. When we align ourselves with the energy of the seventh chakra, we experience synchronicity in our lives. Its behavior drives us to seek to know more about our purpose in life, and its energy lovingly pushes us to reach the full realization of our inborn talents. The seventh chakra is the source of enlightenment and inspiration. When we work with its energy, our perspective on life becomes holistic, and we feel a sense of wonderment and awe. It is easier for us to see the big picture and determine our place and role in that picture. We become visionary in our thinking and experience peace and a sense of comfort, knowing that we belong. This chakra encourages us to reach out to others through the unconditional love found in the fourth chakra. We create behavior that attracts people into our lives, and we experience an inner drive and determination that is needed in order for us to turn our dreams into reality. The energy of the seventh chakra encourages the integration of our total personality. It is through the seventh chakra's energy that we are able to access the energy of the six ethereal chakras (eight through thirteen). If we disconnect ourselves from the energy of the seventh chakra, then we experience an identity crisis—we feel a deep spiritual emptiness throughout our entire being. Then, the body begins to die.

Understanding the Interaction of the Seven Major Chakras

The chakra system represents one more way for us to better understand how we function and why we become ill. Chakras bridge the physical and the spiritual, with each of them providing another way to look at how our thoughts and emotions affect us. The interaction between the chakras provides insight into both where and why blockages are occurring. If the body is to remain healthy, then the communication network of the chakra system must remain open, and each chakra must balance and cooperate with the others. If you are having difficulty in your life, look to your personality and your chakras to provide answers. The more you understand each of them, the easier it will be for you to read your body and make the changes needed to restore balance in the subtle energy body and the physical body.

❧

Reflection

Chakras are the spiritual energy centers of our physical bodies.
Each of the seven major chakras vibrates at its own frequency
and is interdependent with each of the others.
When one chakra is out of balance,
the other chakras must compensate accordingly.

Each chakra radiates its own color.
Chakras one through four tie directly to the red,
orange, yellow, and green colors of the personality types.
While there is not a direct physical connection,
chakras provide a window into our energy
flow and to our physical responses.

❧ ❧ ❧

17

Making the Connection Between Chakras and Personality

"All healing of every nature is changing the vibrations from within."
— Edgar Cayce

For years, psychologists have been producing theories based on personality as a means of trying to understand why people display predictable behavioral patterns. Many of these theories have become the foundation for modern-day therapy. From Freud to Jung, Adler to Assagioli, we are presented with different systems that place an emphasis on one aspect of personality or another. For example, Freud relates human behavior to libido (first chakra, red); and Assagioli approaches it from the eastern philosophy of self and will (seventh chakra, violet). In between these two extreme approaches, we find Adler, who believed that our drives relate to our inner insecurities (fourth chakra, green); and Carl Jung, who related our behavior to intuition (sixth chakra, indigo). All of these theorists categorized people's personality types by looking at only one aspect or another.

I found in the development of my own personality theory that the process of categorizing people was indeed risky, because to truly understand human behavior we need to take into account the whole person. We need to see an individual as a complete unit and not their individual parts. Whenever human behavior is categorized, we create a caricature of people that cannot take into account all of the subtle qualities that make them unique. However, by linking the predictable behavioral patterns of personality with the predictable psychological and emotional responses of the chakra system, we add to the ever-growing picture. I have striven to make the four-color personality theory truly represent the total person.

The Four-Color Theory

Each of us has a predominant color that radiates from within our energy system. That color represents our whole personality—all traits and characteristics. The relationship we have with our personality color is crucial to our health and to our perception of ourselves as a whole. By correlating personality type with the chakra system through color, we can look at the human identity from all levels of consciousness. By using this four-color theory, it is only a matter of understanding the nature of the energy system and the chakras; then we can better understand personality. What the four-color theory reveals is that each of the four personality colors has a particular chakra that is consistently accessed for both energy and information. Let me show you what I mean.

The Red Personality

The *red* personality, which relates to the first chakra, also utilizes chakras three and five in order to support their mental functioning and personality needs. Their main focus on life is through the first chakra, whose energy is associated with the physical world. Once the *red* gathers the information from the first chakra, it moves up to the third chakra, whose energy is tied to mental functioning. The combination of these two chakras provides adequate information for the *reds* to make their decisions. When their decision is made, they move to the fifth chakra to express their decisions and make their needs and wants known. Each of these three chakras accessed by the *reds* bears masculine energy, which is positive and active in its charge, and kindles the desire to get things done.

The Orange Personality

The *orange* personality, which relates to the second chakra, also utilizes chakras four and six in order to support mental functioning, personality, and emotional needs. Their main focus is on relationships and fulfilling the needs of others. The second chakra's energy is associated with both of these behavioral patterns. For *oranges* to be effective in their caretaking of others, they access the energy of the fourth chakra, whose energy is associated with unconditional love. Since *orange* personalities are very intuitive in anticipating the needs of others, they flow to their sixth chakra to support the instinctive feelings that originate in the second chakra. Feminine energy, encouraging relationships and cooperation, predominates in the three chakras that *oranges* access.

The Yellow Personality

The *yellow* personality, which relates to the third chakra, also utilizes chakras one, two, and six, in order to support mental functioning and personality needs. In life, they mainly focus through the third chakra, whose energy is associated with the intellect and the ability to solve problems. The third chakra is responsible for the integration of both intuitive and logical thinking skills. Once the third chakra is accessed, the *yellow* goes to the first chakra to gather information through the five senses and take a pulse check of the physical situation. The *yellow* then flows up to the sixth chakra for alignment and activation of right-brain thinking skills. Once the whole-brain thinking process is activated and the information is processed, then the *yellow* goes back to the second chakra for emotional feedback. The *yellow* is the only personality type that can comfortably flex and utilize chakras that are both masculine and feminine in energy. *Yellows* are genetically designed to function this way so they can see situations from two perspectives. This flexibility in thinking enhances their decision-making abilities, which *yellows* pride themselves on.

The Green Personality

The *green* personality, which relates to the fourth chakra, also utilizes chakras two and six in order to support mental functioning and personality needs. Their main focus is on the need to be loved and the need for creativity. The fourth chakra's energy is associated with self-love and the ability to love others. The sixth chakra's energy is associated with creativity and intuition. In any situation, *greens* immediately flow from the fourth chakra to the sixth chakra to provide intuitive messages that will help them in their interaction with the physical world and with others. Greens use their intuitive insight as a means of directing the course of their lives. However, when it comes to love, either of themselves or others, *greens* look to the second chakra for emotional feedback.

In situations involving relationships, *greens* will trust the input of the second chakra over what their intuition is telling them. If the emotional feedback from the second chakra is positive, then *greens* are open and receptive to building relationships. However, if the second chakra feedback is negative, meaning that there is a pattern of emotional hurt and vulnerability, then *greens* will resist the building of relationships. If the emotional feedback is that of guilt, then *greens* tend to stay in relationships that are not in their best interest. Both the fourth and second chakras are emotionally charged and rely on each other to provide feedback that directs the course of relationships. The chakras that the *greens* access are feminine in energy. However, the *green* personality is the only type that will change color and the chakras they utilize when under extreme stress. When stressed, they take on the characteristics of a *red* personality type and function from chakras one, three, and five. These chakras are masculine in energy, which is diametrically opposed to their normal functioning. Operating from masculine energy energetically drains *greens* and weakens their immune system, leaving them susceptible to infection and illness.

The Interaction Between the Seven Major Chakras and Personality

While each personality color interacts with all seven chakras to some extent, it appears that each type relies more on certain chakras to provide feedback that supports their mental functioning and their approach to self and life. The chakra that each color type functions from first determines their weak sites: *red*, first chakra; *orange*, second chakra; *yellow*, third chakra; and *green*, fourth chakra. Each of the secondary chakras and the areas of the body where those chakras are located tends to produce physical symptoms and are subsidiary sites for illness. The chakras that each personality color primarily functions from are more vulnerable to imbalance, malfunction, and the potential for illness. Now let's look at each chakra and its interaction with personality.

First Chakra—Red—Flows Masculine Energy

Location: At the base of the spine in the area between the anus and genitals. It is associated with the reproductive organs.

Physical connection: Immune system, entire spinal column, pelvis, legs, feet, and rectum. Supplies energy to the kidneys and adrenals.

Emotional connection: It is the basic foundation for our personal sense of security, human survival skills, and self-worth (which is measured by materialism and ego).

Mental connection: The need for order, logic, control, and structure. Relies on a five-sensory approach to life. Driven to do what needs to be done. Lives life from an external perspective.

Personality characteristics: Down-to-earth, pragmatic, controlling of both people and environment. Practical, hard-working, pragmatic, non-emotional, dogmatic, and linear in thinking process. Sees things in black and white. Focuses on providing basic human necessities. Task oriented. Anal retentive.

Personality disorders: Multiple personalities, obsessive-compulsive, paranoid, sadistic, and self-destructive.

Positive behavior: Responsible, dependable, consistent, loyal, active, strong-willed, vital, high energy, success oriented. A doer, gets things done. Follows through on commitments. Generous when deemed justified. Cooperative. Leader, delegator.

Negative behavior: Aggressive, negative, volatile, hot-tempered, domineering, argumentative, defensive, egotistical, quick to react, jumps to conclusions, makes decisions without thinking, impatient, obsessively sexual, wants instant gratification, overreacts, hostile. Holds resentment toward others that take and do not give back. Frustration when others waste their time. Continual power struggle with others.

Basic needs: To belong, to fit into societal traditions. Need for home, physical contact, and sensory gratification. Desire for justice, law and order.

Biggest challenges: To expand thinking beyond just facts and logic. To be open and receptive to new ideas. To trust feminine energy. To allow time for play. Learning to depend on others. Taking time for self.

Primary fears: Loss of personal possessions. Fear for personal safety, betrayal, and feelings of being out of control. Fear of being destitute.

Physical dysfunctions: Chronic back pain, sciatica, varicose veins, rectal bowel disorders, autoimmune diseases, hypertension, heart attacks, stroke, depression, tumors and cancers of pelvic area, blood ailments, circulatory problems, and phlebitis. Tendency toward alcoholism.

Second Chakra—Orange—Flows Feminine Energy

Location: In the lower abdomen. Connected to the sacral and prostatic nerve plexus. It is associated with the reproductive glands, lower digestive system, and urinary system.

Physical connection: Reproductive organs (ovaries and testes), prostate, large and small intestine, lumbar and sacral spinal area, appendix, pancreas, kidneys, and bladder.

Emotional connection: The need for relationships with other people and for control over other individuals in order to maintain some sense of power over their environment. This is the emotional aspect of feelings where we house our sexual, financial, and personal power as it relates to our interactions with others. This is where we house emotions relating to desire.

Mental connection: Makes decisions based on emotion, not logic. Sets psychological boundaries on how we will interact with others. Reminds us not to "sell" ourselves to others just to gain control over them.

Personality characteristics: Caretaking, dependable, thoughtful, strong urge to share, to be a part of social support system, strives for personal recognition, needs social contact, emotionally giving, strong desire to help others. Loyal, devoted, considerate, ever-so-helpful. *Oranges* are the most family oriented of all personality types.

Personality disorders: Passive-aggressive, avoidance behavior, psychopathic and sociopathic behavior.

Positive behavior: Optimistic, hospitable, ambitious, receptive to new ideas, warm, friendly. Reaches out to others, financially self-sufficient, social, supportive, expansive, sensitive, sexually receptive, seeks friendships, and builds strong relationships with others.

Negative behavior: Worrier, pessimistic, frets, self-destructive, victim persona, does not care about self or others, emotionally manipulative, selfish. Low self-esteem, lack of self-worth, frustration with others, resentment around having to care for others. Uses health as means of getting attention and sympathy.

Basic needs: Need for social acceptance, to be appreciated and needed, to have a strong support system. Needs approval from others.

Biggest challenges: Not giving away personal power to others in order to attain goals. Not using emotions to manipulate others and control them. To be able to regain sense of control over one's life. To learn to cope with the essential demands of everyday living.

Primary fears: Being emotionally controlled by others, being financially at the mercy of others. Fear of being alone, of abandonment, and of being inadequate.

Physical dysfunctions: Middle and lower back pain, ruptured disks, slipped disks, female disorders, cramps, irritable bowel syndrome, diabetes, pancreatitis, pancreatic cancer, fibroid cysts in uterus, ovarian cysts and cancer, cervical and uterine cancer, impotence, prostate disorders, urinary infections, kidney stones, kidney disorders, bladder cancer, bladder infections, yeast infections, intestinal problems, manic depression, and disorders associated with hormone imbalance. Tendency toward alcoholism and substance abuse.

Third Chakra—Yellow—Flows Masculine Energy

Location: In the solar plexus, the center of the digestive system. It is associated with the adrenal glands and digestive system.

Physical connection: Stomach, lower esophagus, adrenals, spleen, gallbladder, liver, and thoracic spinal area.

Emotional connection: Personal power center, trust of self and others, accepting responsibility for self, personal honor and pride, core of how personality drives interaction with physical world and others. Self-confidence, self-respect, need for perfection.

Mental connection: Acts as the mediator between the conscious mind and the subconscious mind. Utilizes both logical and subjective approaches to decision making. Seeks balance between masculine and feminine energy. Methodical, rational, precise. The chakra where we store all memories, experiences, thoughts, perceptions, and beliefs. Solution oriented; thinks "out-of-the-box."

Personality characteristics: Self-confident, self-reliant, self-made, self-motivated, and self-fulfilled. Believes in self and one's abilities. Prides oneself on intellectual capabilities. Goal oriented, ambitious, motivated by achievement, innovative, visionary, perfectionist, with the ability to generate action. Challenger, independent, interested in learning, seeks new ways to make things better and has the courage to take risks.

Personality disorders: Narcissistic, obsessive-compulsive, antisocial, schizoid.

Positive behavior: Intellectually curious, interested in self-development, deals logically with problems, straightforward, good at organizing, enjoys planning process, seeks challenges. Solution oriented, seeks ways to use creativity, works from cause-and-effect perspective, challenges status quo.

Negative behavior: Uses intimidation as means of getting one's way, acts irrational, becomes illogical, splits hairs, argumentative, critical of self and others, treats others impersonally, rejects ideas. Aloof, lacks tact, uses intellect to create superiority. Verbose, judgmental, overly opinionated, contradictory, unable to express emotions.

Basic needs: To live in an orderly environment, to express heightened sense of individuality, to be competent, to be an expert, to be intellectually challenged, to turn complexity into simplicity.

Biggest challenges: To learn to trust intuition, to get in touch with emotions, and to not feel so different that one cannot fit into society.

Primary fears: Rejection, intimidation, failure, criticism, looking foolish or stupid, failing to meet responsibilities, loss of physical appearance, and fear that others will *discover* fears.

Physical dysfunctions: Arthritis, digestive disorders, ulcers, hiatal hernia, chronic indigestion, reflux, liver cancer, liver disorders, immune system diseases, adrenal disorders, anxiety attacks, gallstones, skin disorders, headaches, intestinal problems.

Fourth Chakra—Green—Flows Feminine/Masculine Energy

Location: In the chest cavity. It is associated with the thymus gland and heart.

Physical connection: Lungs, heart, thymus gland, shoulders, arms, hands, diaphragm, circulatory system, respiratory system, breasts, ribs, and cervical spinal area.

Emotional connection: Represents balance between physical reality and spiritual inner wisdom. Deals with the principle of unity, compassion, sympathy, unconditional love, self-love, and self-esteem. It resonates feelings, working with the second chakra to establish emotional boundaries around love and relationships. Seeks personal fulfillment. Associated with the feelings of joy, happiness, and love. It is the fulcrum point that balances masculine and feminine energy, and the behavior associated with each.

Mental connection: Integrates emotion and intuition into thinking process. Sees life events from a holistic perspective. Uses intuitive insight as a means of providing direction in life and in relationships. Is open and receptive to new ideas. Loves to create. Relies more on right-brain creative thinking than left-brain logical thinking skills.

Personality characteristics: Creative, inspirational, imaginative, holistic in perspective, keen sense of observation, good at reading body language, highly developed sense of intuition, idealistic, humanitarian, romantic, enthusiastic, nurturing.

Personality disorders: Dependent-submissive behavior, passive-aggressive, excessively emotional, and creates behavior to seek attention.

Positive behavior: Good self-esteem, self nurturing, friendly, passionate, compassionate, reaches out to others, seeks to bring out special qualities of others. Wants to share, open to love, open-hearted, forgiving, dedicated, enjoys healing self and others.

Negative behavior: Feels unworthy of love. Deceitful, insecure, submissive, self-doubting, envious, possessive, jealous, distrustful, fickle, volatile, deceptive, out of touch with reality, impulsive, manipulative, self-destructive.

Basic needs: To feel loved; to have supportive, caring, and nurturing relationships. To feel special and to be creative.

Biggest challenges: To love without creating dependency, to conquer possessiveness, to master self-doubt and to not always see everything as one's own fault.

Primary fears: Fear of not being loved, of being alone. Fear surrounding commitments, being emotionally vulnerable, inability to protect heart and emotions, personal rejection, and being treated impersonally.

Physical dysfunctions: Heart disease, heart attack, mitral valve pro-lapse, circulatory problems, asthma, chronic respiratory disorders, fibroid cysts in breast, breast cancer, allergies, pneumonia, upper back and neck spinal problems, chronic neck and shoulder muscle tension, hormone imbalances, thyroid problems, migraine headaches, neurological disorders, attention deficit disorder, and sus-ceptibility to viral infections.

Fifth Chakra—Red, Orange, Yellow, Green— Flows Masculine Energy

Location: In the throat area. It is associated with the thyroid gland, muscular system, and cerebrospinal nervous system.

Physical connection: Thyroid and parathyroid glands, trachea, upper esophagus, medulla oblongata, brain stem and cervical spine, mouth, jaw, teeth and gums.

Emotional connection: Related to nurturing of self and personal cre-ativity. Represents the power of choice. Its energy is connected with artistic endeavor, speaking, teaching, writing, and the expression of true divine self and willpower.

Mental connection: The challenge of exercising one's willpower. This is the chakra from which we express our choices, make our needs and wants known, and assist energetically in the dialogue between the third and sixth chakras.

Personality characteristics: Introversion and extroversion.

Positive behavior: Ability to speak up for self, assertive. Voice is strong, easy to hear, eloquent, articulate. Able to use words to inspire and provoke strong emotions. Faith, self-knowledge, and personal authority. Capacity to make choices based on needs and wants and to adhere to those choices even if others may not agree.

Negative behavior: Timid, weak voice, submissive undertones in voice, unwillingness to speak up. Lack of assertiveness, lack of faith in self, whiny, fanatical, rigid.

Basic needs: To attain inner peace and live a life where one is true to self.

Primary fears: Not having authority or power of choice. Fears loss of willpower, not being heard. Fears speaking out and conflict that arises out of others disagreeing with our choices or our words. Fear of sounding stupid.

Physical dysfunctions: Laryngitis, raspy throat, throat cancer, hypothyroidism, hyperthyroidism, thyroid cancer, esophageal cancer, mouth ulcers, gum disorders, teeth problems, muscular dystrophy, TMJ (jaw misalignment), swollen lymph glands in neck, tension headaches, scoliosis, Parkinson's disease, paralysis of vocal cords, neurological disorders.

❦

Our interaction with the sixth and seventh chakras is at a more subtle level. While each of the four personality colors may not flow or rely on these chakras as part of their mental functioning or the processing of information, each one accesses and uses its energy and information every moment of our lives. While none of them access it directly, they all access it indirectly.

Sixth Chakra—Flows Feminine Energy

Location: In the brow area of the forehead. It is associated with the pituitary gland.

Physical connection: Brain, autonomic nervous system, central nervous system, pituitary gland, hypothalamus, cerebellum, ears, nose, and eyes.

Emotional connection: Allows us to connect with our inner wisdom. Provides intuitive insight and messages. It is the catalyst that allows us to creatively explore our spiritual world and the truths it contains. It brings together judgment and discrimination. It is the spiritual/emotional aspect of our being. It has no boundaries or limitations with respect to what we are capable of achieving. It encourages the seeking of truth, and using all of our inherent talents. It inspires us to reach beyond the blockages we carry emotionally and psychologically.

Mental connection: It is our intuitive right-brain knowledge center. It links our mental body, our intellectual self, and our personality traits with characteristics. It combines what we have learned with what we believe in. It integrates the thinking of the right and left brains and acts as the communication linkage between the spiritual body and the physical body. It is where we house our emotional intelligence.

Positive behavior: Activates our openness to see situations as lessons that lead us to wisdom. It is understanding at the deepest level. Introspective, curious, interested in learning and growing, provides the ability to use higher reasoning skills, ability to see the big picture and to trust intuitive insights and accept them as real. Openness to the creation of ideas of others. Searches for purpose in life, trusts spirit, is optimistic about the future, and comfortably integrates the sixth sense with the five senses.

Negative behavior: Loses touch with reality, unwillingness to look within, feelings of inadequacy, inability to use imagination and creativity, overbearing, unable to cope with the present. Anxious, fearful of the future, always expecting the worst, overly protective of self and others. Forgetful, argumentative, irresponsible, unpredictable, flighty, and unable to make things happen.

Basic needs: To feel connected to the higher source; to have a purpose in life; and to have relationships that are supportive and that encourage individuality, introspection, and personal growth.

Biggest challenges: Trusting that something is what it is, and accepting it as true. To manifest one's desires instead of just wishing, and to bring dreams into fruition.

Primary fears: Not being able to find one's truth. Fear of not making sound judgments, of relying on external input. Fear of inner weaknesses and of not finding a place to fit into society.

Physical dysfunctions: Brain tumors, brain hemorrhages, strokes, neurological disorders, sleep disorders, pituitary gland tumors, seizures, epilepsy, Alzheimer's disease, blindness, tinnitus, diabetes, deafness, learning disabilities, depression, and schizophrenia.

Seventh Chakra—Flows Feminine and Masculine Energy

Location: At the top of the head (crown). It is associated with the pineal gland and the immune system.

Physical connection: It is where the life force of the divine energy enters our body. This energy nourishes the body, mind, and spirit. It connects all chakras and distributes energy throughout the entire body. It influences all of the body's systems: nervous, energy, skeletal, muscular, respiratory, circulatory, digestive, and immune. Its energy also affects the skin.

Emotional connection: It is our connection with our spiritual nature, and our capacity to integrate such into our physical world. It is the portal to universal knowledge. It contains energy that creates devotion, prophetic thoughts, and mystical connections. This chakra is directly aligned to understanding our relationship with God. It is where we emotionally go to be "one with our Creator." It is our grace and prayer center and is responsible for activating our inner healer.

Mental connection: It contains information needed to help us understand the meaning of life. It contains the purest form of energy that flows through our bodies. It brings clarity to our thinking and helps us to see life on a grander scale. It provides spiritual insight and is part of that mystical realm of the paranormal. It determines the standards we aspire to and maintains alignment with our belief system.

Positive behavior: Imaginative, introspective, peaceful, magical, inspirational. Assists in the making of positive choices, displays strength of character, creates a sense of wonderment, allows us to see the world through a different set of eyes, and encourages us to explore the inner depths of our individuality.

Negative behavior: Self-centered, temperamental, negative self-image, closed-minded, feeling that life is out of control, has identity crises, impractical, spaced out. Feelings of being lost, restless, of being hollow inside. Lack of desire for personal growth, resistant to change, loses touch with reality if there is an absence of faith.

Basic needs: To bring order out of chaos, to integrate God into our everyday lives, to see ourselves as having a place in the grand scheme of life.

Biggest challenges: To be disciplined in manifestation, to transform self-image. To be willing to grow and change in order to flex and learn from life's challenges.

Primary fears: Being alone, spiritual abandonment, loss of identity, loss of connection with loved ones, and the fear of looking inside.

Physical dysfunctions: General overall energy loss, chronic fatigue, severe depression leading to thoughts of suicide. Genetic disorders, multiple sclerosis, ALS (Lou Gehrig's disease), Hodgkin's disease, bone degeneration, bone cancer, extreme sensitivity to light and sound.

Personality Mapping

What this method of linking personality with chakras provides is an accurate way of mapping personality and its overlapping drives. Furthermore, by linking the chakras with personality, it is easier to understand a person's relationship to their physical world, their intuitive world, their relationship with themselves, their sense of certainty or insecurity, and their psychological functioning that affects the endocrine system. By connecting personality with the chakras, we create a comprehensive model of how our mental functioning, thoughts, and emotions affect our health and specific sites within the body. It also allows us to see why each type has a predisposition for certain kinds of illnesses—and the reason those illnesses surface in particular sites of the body.

🜛

Reflection
Each personality color has a primary chakra-related weak site,
and secondary chakras that serve as subsidiary locations
in which symptoms and illnesses can materialize.

Our vulnerability to imbalances of specific types can be related
directly to our personalities and their connections to our primary
and secondary weak sites.

🜛 🜛 🜛

18

The Ethereal Chakras

"Man is in the process of changing to forms of light that are not of this world;
Grows he in time to the formless, a plane on the cycle above.
Know ye must become formless before ye are one with the light."
— The Emerald Tablets (Tablet 8)

We are entering a time of great change. A major shift is taking place. Something is different, and almost everyone is feeling it. We are talking about it, often struggling with it, and seeking to understand it. There is a low level of anxiety that many of us are contending with, and that anxiety is affecting us physically. We're trying to figure out in our own way how to maintain a sense of balance and control in our lives while we feel somewhat out of control. Our old patterns of behavior and thinking are no longer serving us well, so we are being forced to shift our ways of thinking. Those shifts are eroding the foundations on which we have built our perceptions, beliefs, and value systems. Many are struggling to make ends meet financially. Job security is no longer the norm, and our minds are suffering from information overload. There is no denying that this is a time of unprecedented change, and those changes are affecting us all.

While it is the nature of human beings to think that we have control over almost everything, many of the changes and shifts we are experiencing are actually beyond our control. Science has been following earth magnetics, the shifting of the earth's polarities, and the changing of the earth's energy grids for years. New scientific research is showing that significant changes are occurring on Earth. Obvious indicators are the weather patterns and the increase in earthquake activity throughout the world. If you are familiar with basic physiology, you will recall that the body is electrical in nature. It is comprised of billions of cells that are in a constant state of activity working to maintain balance. The reflection of that activity is the human energy system. Each time there is a change in earth's magnetics, every cell in our body must readjust its activity and biochemistry in such a way that it can regain balance and sustain itself. Even subtle changes in nature have a dramatic effect on the energy system, our physical body, our thinking, and the behavior we create to deal with those changes. It's almost as if, every time there is a change, all the parts of us must relearn how to connect and communicate with the others. Fortunately, the reconnecting process does not take long; however, it does take its toll.

In the last three years, I have seen how these changes are affecting our state of mind and, consequently, the health of our bodies. The level of stress that most people are dealing with is energetically draining. It is weakening our immune systems and putting a tremendous amount of wear and tear on our physical bodies. I am seeing a greater potential for the breakdown in communication between the chakras and the endocrine system. This breakdown creates an imbalance in the chemistry of the body and makes us more susceptible to illness and infection. I am hearing more people state that imbalance or malfunctions surround them. They are complaining of having fuzzy thinking, chronic fatigue, sleep deprivation, and a lack of enthusiasm for life. They are saying that they need a break, they are sick and tired, life is hard, they need to get a grip on life, and they just want to be left alone. Each of these statements indicates a particular state of mind, and even more important, what is happening in their bodies.

At the same time, I have actually seen changes in the frequencies and energy patterns of the seven major chakras that are having a significant effect on the physical body. What I am seeing is that chakras one, two, and three are having to work harder to adjust in order to maintain their frequency pattern and coherency. All of the changes are causing the energy of these three chakras to become frenzied. There is a distortion in the way these chakras are communicating with each other, and that distortion is becoming chronic. These three chakras are not able to reestablish communication in such a way that they can regain, or for that matter, maintain balance. The patterns and colors all blend together, muddy the aura, and change a person's behavior. There is mental confusion—emotions seem to be out of control, tempers are running high, and anger and frustration are creating tremendous amounts of stress.

I am seeing a greater number of first, second, and third chakra illnesses than I did three years ago. This frenzied activity in the lower chakras is putting more demand and stress on the fourth chakra, whose energy is designed to assist in the balancing and healing of the body. Consequently, fourth chakra illnesses such as immune disorders, heart disease in both men and women, breast cancer, asthma, and even tuberculosis are on the rise. There appears to be an energetic struggle going on in our ability to connect our physical self with our spiritual self. This is reflected in the energy system such that it appears that the person is being torn in half energetically. What I hear is that people are feeling as if they have lost touch with themselves. They feel disconnected, and they express confusion with respect to what spirituality is and how they are to make a connection with God.

In the last two years, I have started seeing another shift occurring in the energy system. It is a positive by-product of what is happening in the lower chakras of the body. That shift in energy is the presence and activation of six additional chakras. These ethereal chakras are not housed within the physical body; their energy is not directly attached to the endocrine glands. They do, however, have a profound effect on the ascension of our thoughts and how our immune system functions to maximize its healing abilities. It appears that out of the chaos resulting from all of this change, a new light is emerging.

Thirteen Chakras

There have been many differing beliefs about the numbers of chakras in the body. The ancient Chinese thought there were only four, while others believe that there are seven or eight. According to the ancient texts of Mayans and Incans, and the metaphysicians of Egyptian times, there are 13 chakras—12 that the spiritual and physical body draw energy and information from, and the 13th being the chakra that aligns us with our divine Creator and a higher source of knowledge. It is the energy of the 13th chakra that inspires spiritual growth, feeds our soul, and allows true healing of body, mind, and spirit.

I work with all 13 chakras in my readings. The seven major chakras housed within the physical body help me better understand people's ailments, and the six ethereal chakras help me better understand where they are in their inner quest for self-understanding. Working with these additional six chakras provides a more comprehensive, sophisticated, and complete picture of where people are energetically. Working with all 13 chakras, it is easier to see and understand the deeper, more subtle blocks that prevent individuals from having the health and life they desire.

Six Ethereal Chakras

Each of us has six ethereal chakras within our energy system. We interact daily with their energy and feel their benefit to some extent. However, most of us are not reaping the full benefit that these chakras offer. I believe the primary reason is lack of awareness of their presence. Secondly, we have not learned how to trust information that does not reveal itself through our five senses. The six ethereal chakras do not dialogue with us in a way that the conscious mind can interpret. The wisdom one receives from these chakras cannot be accessed by a logical, judgmental mind or where limitations are present. The information provided by these chakras is accessible only when the mind is relaxed—that is, in times of quiet introspection.

For each of us to fully benefit from the energy of the six ethereal chakras, we must be willing to let go of the need to control, and take time out of our busy schedules to go within. We must be open, receptive, and willing to surrender unconditionally to a higher source. We must believe in our mind and heart that every experience we live is the opportunity for us to become better acquainted with who we really are. That challenge is a chance to learn and get one step closer to fulfilling our sacred contract. In these tumultuous times where change is happening at an accelerated pace, we are offered that opportunity. The six chakras can tell us how.

I would like to introduce you to these six ethereal chakras and briefly describe their function. In doing so, it is not my desire to convince you of their presence, but to merely bring forth an awareness of them. I believe that all illness results simply from imbalance, and once that imbalance is clarified, then we can make the appropriate modifications to regain it. Each of us can begin now to reconstruct ourselves in such a way that we are better equipped to live with the challenges that life presents us. Each of us can learn how to tap into the light force that can bring true healing to our body and mind.

Chakras Eight Through Thirteen

Chakras eight, nine, and thirteen have to do with our spiritual ascension. Chakras ten, eleven, and twelve have to do with the health of the body and the strengthening of the immune system.

The Eighth Chakra—This chakra is located three to six inches off the left side of the crown of the head. The energy of the eighth chakra does not influence the health of the physical body, nor does it directly impact the psychological functioning of the brain or alter our emotional behavior. This chakra is our archive of information pertaining to our lives, both past and present. It is a microfiche of our Akashic records. This is the chakra I access to bring forth past-life information in my sessions. If you do not believe in past lives, look at the information stored in this chakra as a representation of your archetypal patterns of behavior as described by Carl Jung.

Until recently, meaning within the last few years, it has not been as important for us to access the information stored within this chakra. However, as we enter the Aquarian Age, the need to understand ourselves better and more deeply is becoming increasingly evident. The information of the eighth chakra surfaces in the symbolism of our dreams and can be accessed through past-life regression.

The Ninth Chakra—The ninth chakra is located three to six inches off the right side of the crown of the head. As with the eighth chakra, this chakra does not influence physical health or psychological functioning. It does, however, influence one's thoughts and emotions. Once a person expands their thinking to include the ninth chakra, their thoughts and perceptions of the world and their place in it take on a new meaning. Their hearts open up to themselves and others. Housed within this chakra is information from a higher source. It is like the great library for universal thinking, and within it resides the keys to higher understanding. Mystics refer to the knowledge we access through this chakra as that of the fourth dimension. It is through the ninth chakra that we seek answers beyond those which our rational minds can provide. We can only access its information through our sixth sense. This chakra has been called by many names from one civilization to another. It has been referred to as the Council of Elders; the Galactic Council of Twelve; the Room of Sages; the House of the Seven Lords; and in the Emerald Tablets of Egyptian times, it was called the Halls of Amenti.

The Tenth Chakra—This chakra is located directly over the crown of the head and forms the shape of a funnel, through which all energy flows from the heavens to the earth, thus supporting the belief, "As above, so be it below." As the energy of the tenth chakra enters the physical body, it flows through the pranic tube that runs down the entire body. The word *prana* refers to life force, or energy. The pranic tube is about two inches in diameter, but it does not follow the curve of the spine, nor is its energy attached directly to any of the seven chakras housed within the physical body. However, its energy influences the functioning and balance of the seven chakras. The energy that flows through the tenth chakra is pure healing energy and contains the frequencies of all thirteen chakras, both the seven housed within the body, and the six ethereal chakras. When we access the energy of the tenth chakra, we stabilize both the energy of the chakras and the endocrine system of the body. It adjusts all imbalances, creating the perfect environment for healing, and even spontaneous remission, to occur.

How do we tap into the energy of the tenth chakra? We must begin through the energy of the fourth chakra by learning to love ourselves for who we are. Next, we need to tap into the sixth chakra and allow the mind to be free of limited thinking. Finally, we need to open up the seventh chakra by asking for guidance from the divine to assist us in our journey to self-understanding and enlightenment.

The Eleventh Chakra—The energy of the eleventh chakra rides over the left shoulder. Though its energy is not physically housed in the body, it aligns itself with the fourth chakra of the heart. The energy of this chakra directly affects the health and vitality of the physical body; however, it does not affect psychological functioning or emotions. The fourth chakra as a stand-alone chakra is masculine in energy, yet in order for it to perform its primary function of adding balance back to the body, it must first be balanced itself. The eleventh chakra creates that balance by adding feminine energy. When these two energies merge, the heart becomes neutral in its energetic polarity. The energy of the eleventh chakra also acts as a booster system for the fourth when it becomes depleted. The stress being created in the fourth chakra by the frenzied energy of the first, second, and third chakras validates the important role the eleventh chakra plays. The energy of the eleventh adds vitality back into the body and stabilizes and harmonizes the frequencies of all of the chakras. It allows us to connect the energy of our lower physical chakras (first, second, and third), with the energy of our upper spiritual chakras (fifth, sixth, and seventh) through the fourth chakra without the fourth becoming ill.

The Twelfth Chakra—The energy of the twelfth chakra rides over the right shoulder. As with the eleventh chakra, its energy, though not physically housed in the body, is aligned with the spleen (third chakra). The spleen is crucial to the functioning of the immune system and the body's ability to fight off infection and disease. As the hub of the immune system's activity, it is responsible for the production of white blood cells and the removal of unwanted debris from the blood. The activity of the spleen coordinates its efforts with the lymphatic system, the thymus gland, and the liver. The pineal gland (seventh chakra), is believed to be the chemical regulator of the immune system's activity.

The twelfth chakra's energy is unique in many ways. First, the influence that its energy has on the immune system as a whole increases vitality, so we can remain healthy even with all of the wear and tear occurring within the body from the stress of life. Second, its energy is housed in the shape of a small pyramid. While the energy of the other chakras tends to be circular in movement, the energy from the twelfth moves from point to point within the pyramid. The pyramid shape symbolizes the connection between body, mind, and spirit. In the twelfth chakra, it represents the connection between the pituitary and pineal glands (central nervous system), spleen (immune system), and adrenals (endocrine system). When all of these systems work in a balanced, coordinated effort, then the body is truly able to heal and benefit fully from the healing energy of the tenth chakra.

The Thirteenth Chakra—The energy of this chakra swirls over the crown and around the entire body, affecting all aspects of our being: spiritual, emotional, mental, and physical. The key to activation is in the asking, for this energy is omnipresent. When we call on this energy, it flows from the crown, down the funnel of the tenth chakra, and then through the pranic tube, energizing all seven chakras of the physical body. Charged with hope and love, it makes us feel optimistic about the future, and changes our attitudes toward life. We are no longer inhibited by limitations of thought or the boundaries of our emotions. Its energy is also neutral in polarity. When we connect with the divine energy at this level of consciousness, we create a perfect state of "spiritual androgyny;" we are able to access masculine and feminine energy equally. This way, we may transcend to a higher, more divine sense of self—the self that is capable of creating miracles.

As we move into the 21st century, the Aquarian Age, these six ethereal chakras will play an even more significant role in our ability to maintain balance and heal ourselves. The collective energy that these chakras offer encourages us to unlock the mysteries that lie within our subconscious minds and to look at every change as though we were either seeing it for the first or last time. When we do so, we will always see change as an opportunity to grow. By integrating the energy of the six ethereal chakras with the seven physical chakras, we will be able to find the keys to help unlock those mysteries. We will align ourselves with the light, and we will tap into our most powerful healing force—the healing energy of hope.

※

Reflection
Chakras eight through thirteen require us to accept both ancient and contemporary perspectives that we are spiritual beings subject to the influence of the ethereal.

These chakras serve as our gateway to the Aquarian Age and our access to the depths of our subconscious minds, where wisdom has no boundaries.

※ ※ ※

19

The Healing Energy of Hope

"Hope is a thing with feathers that perches in the soul, and
sings the tune without the words and never stops at all."
— Emily Dickinson

While it is true that the physical body is always in a state of self-renewal and is capable of healing itself when it becomes stressed, distressed, or chemically or energetically out of balance, it always needs help. Each of us is responsible for the health and well-being of our body, and each of us is instrumental in how it heals and how quickly it does so. The ability to heal ourselves is inherent. Healing in its broadest and most permanent sense means creating the harmonious interaction of activity between the body, mind, and spirit. Healing is the progressive process of revitalization and rejuvenation and is not just about treating symptoms or even the eradication of disease from the body, but about creating balance and eliminating the causes of imbalance. It requires cooperative work between our thoughts and the resultant emotional reactions to maintain balance in the physical body. Basically, healing requires us to create balance between our heads and our hearts.

When it comes to healing ourselves, we each possess a powerful source of healing energy that we can access anytime. This healing energy can restore balance and change the chemistry of our body to promote good health. Unfortunately, we often forget to call on its energy until we are in times of need or we become ill. What I am referring to is *"the healing energy of hope."* Hope and the energy it creates is our greatest weapon in the battle with illness and in overcoming pessimism and emotional despair. I have discovered, especially working with people who have been diagnosed with chronic illness, that the one thing that triggers the healing reaction faster and causes true healing to occur is the presence of hope. Without it, the body struggles to regain a sense of balance, and the healing process is inhibited—that is, we actually lose energy and weaken our immune system. Our resistance to disease and infection is greatly reduced. With the presence of hope, our energy system is strong, our physical body remains healthy and vital, our ability to adjust to life's challenges increases, our stress level decreases, and our immune system is strengthened. If we would only remember that when it comes to good health, our best medicine truly is hope.

But what is hope? The dictionary defines it as "a desire, accompanied by the belief of fulfillment." I define it as "the energy that adds the rainbow to the aura." It is the healing energy created when we align ourselves with the divine higher source of light (the 13th chakra). Hope offers the reassurance that we have a purpose in life. Its energy comforts us and reminds us that we are not alone in a world that often feels intimidating and hostile. Hope influences the way we look at life, how we think, play, and respond to our external world. It is the singular mode of perceiving life that changes both the energy and chemistry of the body. Its energy is both preventive and curative.

Let me tell you about my session with Mary to help you better understand how powerful the energy of hope is in the healing process.

Mary—Age 42

From the first time that I connected with Mary energetically, I knew there was something special about her, and that she had a very important task to accomplish in her lifetime. Yet, when she walked through my door, I could instantly see the severity with which cancer was ravaging her body. Her body was riddled with disease, and her posture reflected how tired her body was from having to work so hard just to keep functioning. Her overall energy field was weak and depleted, and her aura had huge, colorless voids in it. The colors and energy patterns I see when cancer is present overpowered all of the other colors in her energy field. I thought about how paradoxical life can be in the way that it chooses to remind us of what we came here to do. My pre-session preparation told me that Mary was not coming to see me to explain the status of her health. So I began the session by asking her if she had been diagnosed yet. She said she had. She was told she had a terminal blood disease and that she might live up to six months.

I shared my sense that we did not need to spend time with the explanation of the illness itself. She agreed. I then asked her to provide some guidance on how I could be of the most value to her. She said that if this is how she was to die, then so be it. However, before she died she had a lot to do. She *hoped* I could help her better understand what that something was. She wanted a sense of what, if anything, she had to do to tie up spiritual loose ends. Also, she wanted to be sure that, if she was being given this six-month window of opportunity, she take full advantage of it by honoring herself and her spirit. As we talked about life and sacred contracts, it was hard to remember that she was diagnosed as "terminal." Her enthusiasm for what she loved was contagious, and her sense of humor was marvelous. We talked about dying as if we were preparing a meal. She truly had no fear or remorse over how she had lived her life.

I asked Mary what she wanted to do before she died. She began discussing *hopes:* that she would see her daughter get married in eight months; that she would see the birth of her first grandchild who was due in six months; that she and her husband would take off a couple of weeks after the wedding and go to Hawaii—a lifelong dream of hers; that she could live her last few months without being bedridden and without being a burden to her family. She *hoped* she could have the energy to plant her spring flowers and be around long enough to see them bloom. She *hoped* that she could do what she felt in her heart she came into this lifetime to do. As Mary talked about the future and her many *hopes*, I could see this faint light of energy deep within her spiritual energy layer. I know this light well. It is the light that reflects the energy of hope. The more Mary talked about the future, the more vivid and colorful her light energy of hope became.

We talked about putting a plan in place that she could work with month to month to keep her focused on the future. I encouraged her to seek whatever traditional medicine and alternative methods she was comfortable with in order to put a healing program in place that could potentially extend her life. I suggested that she take up activities that she had always wanted to try. Mary decided that she wanted to put together a six-month plan of action. Then if she lived beyond those six months, she would put together another six-month plan. Mary made the decision to change whatever she had to in order to extend her life. She said she was determined to live beyond the six months and felt that the healing energy of hope would help her do it.

I heard from Mary six months after our initial session. She said she wanted to come in and have what she called a "Hope Light Checkup." She now calls me every six months to report on her progress and to get her checkup. Not only is Mary now two and one-half years beyond when she was told she would die, she is actually getting better. As part of her six-month plan of action, she gets her blood checked, and instead of her cancer getting worse, it appears to be in remission. Her body is learning how to rebuild itself and is progressively showing signs of getting stronger.

When people ask Mary what she did that changed her life and turned her illness around, she tells them she gave up a lot of bad habits, put together a good game plan for living the lifestyle she wanted, and added the word *hope* to her vocabulary. Through adversity and the challenges that life put on her path, Mary finally found her purpose. She has become a hospice volunteer and counsels people to plan for the future, one day at a time. She inspires others by being a living example of how the healing energy of hope can make the impossible, possible. She teaches people how to turn their hope light on and keep it glowing every day.

The Power of Hope

Recent studies in the field of neurochemistry show that there is an area in the brain that responds chemically to the positive feelings that hope triggers. That area is the thalamus. When this part of the brain is stimulated, it produces endorphins, morphinelike substances that seek out and lock into specific receptor sites within the brain. These endorphins tell the mind and body to "feel better." When the mind gets that message, it relays electrochemical signals throughout the body that tell the body to relax and to feel better. At the same time, it also sends electrical impulses to the autonomic nervous system and tells it to return to its natural rhythmic patterns so the body can restore balance. The tangible result we experience from this neurophysiological processing is that our thoughts turn to optimism, and we develop a positive attitude toward life.

Optimism—What Hope Inspires

We are designed to be optimistic beings. It is part of our survival instinct and central in the process of our evolution. Optimism is the attitude we create when we decide to change our way of thinking and the way we look at life. When the energy created from optimism is combined with the energy of hope, it strengthens our immune system. It encourages us to reach beyond our self-perceived limitations and produces an overall feeling of well-being throughout the body. Optimism inspires us to accomplish things that, if left to the conscious mind, would seem impossible. Optimism keeps us motivated when our courage is lacking and when our burdens seem insurmountable. It challenges us to expand our thinking and look to the future, and helps us cope with life, handle physical pain, deal with emotional devastation, push forward even in the face of adversity, and conquer our fears. It is even believed to intervene and prevent decay of the body through the normal life cycles.

When we have hope and optimism in our lives, our attitude toward life cannot be anything but positive. And, when it comes to sustaining good health, a positive attitude is everything. Let me share a story a client sent me following our session where we talked about the importance of hope, optimism, and a positive attitude.

Sandy's Story

Sandy was the kind of person you would love to hate. She was always in a good mood and always had something positive to say. When asked how she was doing, she would always reply, "If I felt any better, I wouldn't know what to do with myself."

Sandy was a young, single mother of three small children. She had spent much of her adult life on welfare, but she had always hoped to find a good-paying job so she could be self-sufficient. Determined to make her desire come true, she made the commitment to go back to school and get her high school diploma. At the same time, she was working in a fast-food restaurant while caring for the needs of her family.

Sandy was a unique person because even without really having anything, people always seemed to be drawn to her. They liked her attitude toward life and her determination. She motivated people. If she sensed that someone was having a bad day, she would say something cheerful and encourage them to look at the positive side of life.

When people would ask her how she could be so happy, considering the pressure she was under, she would reply, "When I wake up in the morning, I first give thanks for waking up. Then I say to myself, *Sandy, you have two choices today. You can choose to be in a good mood and thankful for what you have, or you can be in a bad mood and feel sorry for yourself.* I always choose to be in a good mood, because when I tried being in a bad mood, and felt sorry for myself, I never got anywhere. And, besides that, I was always sick. I decided then and there that I would choose the positive side of life. When I am in a good mood and something bad happens, I see it as a choice. I can either choose to be a victim or I can choose to learn from it. To me, life is about choices. When you cut away all the fluff from life, every situation presents a choice. You choose how you react to situations, you choose how you let people affect you, and you choose your mood."

One night, Sandy was working late and was closing up the restaurant when three men forced their way in at gunpoint. Sandy had always been told to cooperate and give robbers whatever they wanted. As she was trying to give them the money, one of the robbers panicked at the sound of something, and his gun went off, hitting Sandy in the chest. Luckily, someone heard the shot, and she was rushed to the hospital.

After several hours of surgery and a few weeks in intensive care, Sandy was finally released from the hospital. As soon as she was able, she was back at school and back at her job. When her old customers saw her, they were amazed that she came back to work at the restaurant and that she was still her positive old self. When they asked how she was, she replied, "If I felt any better, I wouldn't know what to do with myself." The customers were curious about what went through her mind when she was being robbed. She said, "The first thing was that I probably should have been more careful. Then as I laid there on the floor, I remembered I had two choices: I could choose to live so I could fulfill my dreams and see my kids grow up, or I could choose to die. I chose to live—I was scared, but I knew I had to live."

Sandy said that she could remember everyone telling her in the ambulance that she was going to be fine. But when she got to the hospital and saw the expressions on the doctors' and nurses' faces, then she really got scared. She said she knew she had to take action. She remembers all of the activity, and one nurse asking her if she was allergic to anything. She said, "Yes, bullets. And I am choosing to live, so please work on me as if I am going to live." The last thing she remembered was hearing them laugh.

Sandy lived, thanks to the skill of the hospital staff. In her case, it was also because optimism and a positive attitude saved her life.

Making Our Choices

As I read this story, I thought back and reflected on the choices I'd made that changed the course of my life forever. I still remember well what my light friends shared with me: Life really is about choices and hope. Optimism and a positive attitude play an important role in the choices we make. Our lives should be our candy store, filled with scrumptious goodies, and our choices should be how to best invest our limited resources. When we get right down to it, the choices we make determine the quality of our lives and the quality of our health.

🐝

Reflection
Hope is the fuel that powers us.
It is the impetus that keeps us moving when our bodies tire,
when our enthusiasm lags, and when our burdens become overwhelming.
Hope is a choice. Hope may not guarantee happiness and wellness,
but without it, prospects fade rapidly.

Wellness is directly connected to our immune system,
which responds to hope and the positive energy it creates.

🐝 🐝 🐝

WELLNESS BEGINS WITH YOU

I n this book, I have attempted to introduce a new theory on why we become ill. My intention in doing so is to help you better understand yourself—to see why you think and act as you do. If you look at your personality and link it with the information contained within your energy system and your chakras, you will have a comprehensive new way of looking at yourself. I hope that I have aroused your curiosity enough that you will look even deeper within so you can recognize which thoughts, emotions, and habits are preventing you from enjoying the life and health you desire. Ralph Waldo Emerson said, "What lies behind us and what lies before us are small matters compared to what lies within us." If you remember that everything you need to know lies within you, then you can choose to use that information to make a difference in your life.

I wish you well on your journey toward self-understanding, on your inner quest to find balance, and on your search for good health and happiness.

May the light of your hope shine brightly, and may your life be filled with health, joy, and contentment.

🐾 🐾 🐾

APPENDIX

BIBLIOGRAPHY

Albrecht, Karl, *Brain Power*, Englewood Cliffs, NJ: Prentice Hall, 1980.

Amber, Reuben, *Color Therapy*, New York: Aurora Press, 1983.

Assagioli, Roberto, *Psychosynthesis: A Manual of Principles and Techniques*, New York: Viking Press, 1971.

Babbit, Edwin, *The Principles of Light and Color*, New York: Citadel Press, 1967.

Bailey, Alice A., *Esoteric Healing*, New York: Lucis Publishing, 1953.

Berkow, Robert, *The Merck Manual of Diagnosis and Therapy*, West Point, PA: Merck Sharp & Dohme International, 1982.

Birren, Faber, *Colour Psychology and Colour Therapy*, New York: Citadel Press, 1950.

——, *Colour and the Human Response*, New York: Reinhold Publishing, 1970.

Bowers, Barbara, Ph.D., *What Color Is Your Aura?*, New York: Pocket Books, 1989.

Brennan, Barbara Ann, *Hands of Light*, New York: Bantam Books, 1987.

——, *Light Emerging*, New York: Bantam Books, 1993.

Bruyere, Roslyn L., *Wheels of Light*, Arcadia, CA: Bon Productions, 1989.

Cayce, Edgar, *Individual Reference File*, Virginia Beach, VA: A.R.E. Press, 1970.

——, *A Search for God Book I*, Virginia Beach, VA: A.R.E. Press, 1942.

——, *Auras*, Virginia Beach, VA: A.R.E. Press, 1945.

Chin, Richard, M.D., *The Energy Within*, New York: Marlowe & Company, 1995.

Doreal, M., *The Emerald Tablets of Thoth-the-Atlantean*: Alexandrian Library Press.

Ferguson, Marilyn, *The Brain Revolution*, New York: Bantam Books, 1975.

——, *The Aquarian Conspiracy*, Los Angeles, CA: J.P. Tarcher, Inc., 1980.

Frager, Roger and James Fadiman, *Personality & Personal Growth*, New York: Harper Collins Publishers, 1984.

Haray, Keith, M.D., and Eileen Donahue, *Who Do You Think You Are?*, New York: Harper Collins, 1994.

Hay, Louise L., *You Can Heal Your Life*, Carlsbad, CA: Hay House, Inc., 1984.

Hills, Christopher, *Nuclear Evolution*, Boulder Creek, CA: University of the Trees Press, 1977.

Hills, Norah, *You Are A Rainbow*, Boulder Creek, CA: University of the Trees Press, 1979.

Hurley, Kathleen and Theodore Dobson, *My Best Self*, New York: Harper Collins, 1993.

Jones, Alex, *Seven Mansions of Color*, Marina Del Rey, CA: Devorss & Company, 1982.

Jung, Carl, *Man and His Symbols*, New York: Dell Publishing Co., 1964.

——, *Psychological Types*, Princeton, NJ: Princeton University Press, 1971.

Karagulla, Dr. Shafica and Dora van Gelder Kunz, *The Chakras and the Human Energy Fields*, London: Theosophical Publishing House, 1989.

Kargere, Audrey, *Color and Personality*, York Beach, ME: Samuel Weiser, Inc., 1982.

Keirsey, David and Marilyn Bates, *Please Understand Me*, Del Mar, CA: Prometheus Nemesis, 1978.

Leadbeater, C.W., *The Chakras*, London: Theosophical Publishing House, 1974.

Lewis, Roger, *Color and the Edgar Cayce Readings*, Virginia Beach, VA: A.R.E. Press, 1973.

Luscher, Max, *The 4-Color Person*, New York: Simon & Schuster, 1977.

McGarey, William, M.D., *In Search of Healing*, New York: The Berkley Publishing Group, 1996.

Olda, John, M.D., and Lois Morris, *Personality Self-Portrait*, New York: Bantam Books, 1990.

Orstein, Robert, M.D., and Cionis Swen, *The Healing Brain*, New York: Guildford Press, 1990.

Ott, John N., *Health & Light*, Columbus, OH: Ariel Press, 1973.

Ouseley, S. G. J., *The Power of the Rays*, London, L. N. Fowler & Co. Ltd., 1951.

Reich, Wilhelm, *Character Analysis*, London: Vision Press, 1950.

Restak, Richard, M.D., *The Brain*, New York: Bantam Books, 1984.

Siegel, Bernie, M.D., *Love, Medicine & Miracles*, New York: Harper & Row, 1986.

Singer, June, *Boundaries of the Soul*, New York: Anchor Books, 1972.

Shealy, Norman C., M.D., and Caroline Myss, *The Creation of Health*, Walpole, NH: Stillpoint Publishing, 1988.

Springer, Sally and George Deutsch, *Left Brain, Right Brain*, San Francisco, CA: W. H. Freeman & Co., 1981.

Surgue, T., *There Is A River: The Story of Edgar Cayce*, Virginia Beach, VA: A.R.E. Press, 1957.

Walker, Morton, M.D., *The Power of Color*, New York: Avery Publishing Group, 1991.

Wonder, Jacquelyn and Pricillia Donovan, *Whole Brain Thinking*, New York: Morrow, 1984.

Zdenek, Marilee, *Right Brain Experience*, New York: McGraw Hill, 1983.

Zukav, Gary, *The Seat of the Soul*, New York: Fireside Books, Simon & Schuster, 1990.

SELF-HELP RESOURCES

The following list of resources can be used for more information about recovery options for addictions, health concerns, death and bereavement, and other issues. The addresses and telephone numbers listed are for the national headquarters; look in your local yellow pages under "Community Services" for resources closer to your area.

In addition to the following groups, other self-help organizations may be available in your area to assist your healing and recovery for a particular life crisis not listed here. Consult your telephone directory, call a counseling center or help line near you, or contact:

Attorney Referral Network
(800) 624-8846

National Self-Help Clearinghouse
25 West 43rd St., Room 620
New York, NY 10036
(800) 952-2075

AIDS

AIDS Hotline
(800) 342-2437

Children with AIDS (CWA) Project of America
(800) 866-AIDS (24-hour hotline)

The Names Project – AIDS Quilt
(800) 872-6263

National AIDS Network
(800) 342-2437

Project Inform
19655 Market St., Ste. 220
San Francisco, CA 94103
(415) 558-8669

PWA Coalition
50 W. 17th St.
New York, NY 10011

Spanish AIDS Hotline
(800) 344-7432

TDD (Hearing Impaired) AIDS Hotline
(800) 243-7889

ALCOHOL ABUSE

Al-Anon Family Headquarters
200 Park Ave. South
New York, NY 10003
(757) 563-1600

Alcoholics Anonymous (AA)
General Service Office
475 Riverside Dr.
New York, NY 10115
(212) 870-3400

Children of Alcoholics Foundation
33 West 60th St., 5th Floor
New York, NY 10023
(212) 757-2100 ext. 6370
(212) 757-2208 (fax)
(800) 359-COAF

Meridian Council, Inc.
Administrative Offices
4 Elmcrest Terrace
Norwalk, CT 06850

Mothers Against Drunk Driving (MADD)
(254) 690-6233

National Association of Children of Alcoholics (NACOA)
11426 Rockville Pike, Ste. 100
Rockville, MD 20852
(301) 468-0985
(888) 554-2627

National Clearinghouse for Alcohol and Drug Information (NCADI)
P.O. Box 234
Rockville, MD 20852
(301) 468-2600

National Council on Alcoholism and Drug Dependency (NCADD)
12 West 21st St.
New York, NY 10010
(212) 206-6770

National Council on Alcohol & Drugs
(800) 475-HOPE

Women for Sobriety
(800) 333-1606

ANOREXIA/BULIMIA

American Anorexia/Bulimia Association, Inc.
293 Central Park West, Ste. 1R
New York, NY 10024
(212) 575-6200

Eating Disorder Organization
6655 S. Yale Ave.
Tulsa, OK 74136
(918) 481-4044

CANCER

National Cancer Institute
(800) 4-CANCER

ECAP (Exceptional Cancer Patients)
Bernie S. Siegel, M.D.
53 School Ground Rd., Unit 3
Branford, CT 06405
(203) 315-3321

CHILDREN'S ISSUES

<u>Child Molestation</u>

Adults Molested As Children United (AMACU)
232 East Gish Rd.
San Jose, CA 95112
(800) 422-4453

National Committee for Prevention of Child Abuse
332 South Michigan Ave., Ste. 1600
Chicago, IL 60604
(312) 663-3520

<u>Children's and Teens' Crisis Intervention</u>

Boy's Town Crisis Hotline
(800) 448-3000

Children of the Night
(800) 551-1300

Covenant House Hotline
(800) 999-9999

Kid Save
(800) 543-7283

National Runaway and Suicide Hotline
(800) 448-3000

Youth Nineline
(Referrals for parents/teens about drugs, homelessness, runaways)
(800) 999-9999

Missing Children

Missing Children—Help Center
410 Ware Blvd., Ste. 400
Tampa, FL 33619
(800) USA-KIDS

National Center for Missing and Exploited Children
1835 K St. NW
Washington, DC 20006
(800) 843-5678

Children with Serious Illnesses (fulfilling wishes)

Brass Ring Society
National Headquarters
551 East Semoran Blvd., Suite E-5
Fern Park, FL 32730
(407) 339-6188
(800) 666-WISH

Make-a-Wish Foundation
(800) 332-9474

CO-DEPENDENCY

Co-Dependents Anonymous
(602) 277-7991

DEATH/GRIEVING/SUICIDE

Grief Recovery Helpline
(800) 445-4808

Grief Recovery Institute
8306 Wilshire Blvd., Ste. 21A
Beverly Hills, CA 90211
(213) 650-1234

National Hospice Organization (NHO)
1901 Moore St. #901
Arlington, VA 22209
(703) 243-5900

National Sudden Infant Death Syndrome
Two Metro Plaza, Ste. 205
Landover, MD 20785
(800) 221-SIDS

Seasons: Suicide Bereavement
P.O. Box 187
Park City, UT 84060
(801) 649-8327

Share
(Recovering from violent death of friend or family member)
100 E 8th St., Suite B41
Cincinnati, OH 45202
(513) 721-5683

Survivors of Suicide
Call your local Mental Health Association for the branch nearest you.

Widowed Persons Service
(202) 434-2260
(800) 424-3410 ext. 2260

DEBTS

Credit Referral
(Information on local credit counseling services)
(800) 388-CCCS

Debtors Anonymous
General Service Office
P.O. Box 400
Grand Central Station
New York, NY 10163-0400
(212) 642-8220

DIABETES

American Diabetes Association
(800) 232-3472

DRUG ABUSE

Cocaine Anonymous
(800) 347-8998

National Cocaine-Abuse Hotline
(800) 262-2463
(800) COCAINE

National Institute of Drug Abuse (NIDA)
Parklawn Building
5600 Fishers Lane, Room 10A-39
Rockville, MD 20852
(301) 443-6245 (for information)
(800) 662-4357 (for help)

World Service Office (CA)
3740 Overland Ave., Ste. C
Los Angeles, CA 90034-6337
(310) 559-5833
(800) 347-8998 (to leave message)

EATING DISORDERS

Eating Disorder Organization
6655 S. Yale Ave.
Tulsa, OK 74136
(918) 481-4044

Overeaters Anonymous
National Office
P.O. Box 44020
Rio Rancho, NM 87174-4020
(505) 891-2664

GAMBLING

Gamblers Anonymous
National Council on Compulsive Gambling
444 West 59th St., Room 1521
New York, NY 10019
(212) 903-4400

HEALTH ISSUES

Alzheimer's Disease Information
(800) 621-0379

American Chronic Pain Association
P.O. Box 850
Rocklin, CA 95677
(916) 632-0922

American Foundation of Traditional Chinese Medicine
505 Beach St.
San Francisco, CA 94133
(415) 776-0502

American Holistic Health Association
P.O. Box 17400
Anaheim, CA 92817
(714) 779-6152

Chopra Center for Well Being
Deepak Chopra, M.D.
7630 Fay Ave.
La Jolla, CA 92037
(619) 551-7788

The Fetzer Institute
9292 West KL Ave.
Kalamazoo, MI 49009
(616) 375-2000

Hippocrates Health Institute
1443 Palmdale Court
West Palm Beach, FL 33411
(561) 471-8876

Hospicelink
(800) 331-1620

Institute for Noetic Sciences
P.O. Box 909, Dept. M
Sausalito, CA 94966-0909
(800) 383-1394

The Mind-Body Medical Institute
185 Pilgrim Rd.
Boston, MA 02215
(617) 632-9525

National Health Information Center
P.O. Box 1133
Washington, DC 20013-1133
(800) 336-4797

Optimum Health Care Institute
6970 Central Ave.
Lemon Grove, CA 91945
(619) 464-3346

Preventive Medicine Research Institute
Dean Ornish, M.D.
900 Bridgeway, Ste. 2
Sausalito, CA 94965
(415) 332-2525

World Research Foundation
20501 Ventura Blvd., Ste. 100
Woodland Hills, CA 91364
(818) 999-5483

HOUSING RESOURCES

Acorn
(Nonprofit network of low- and moderate-income housing)
739 8th St., S.E.
Washington, DC 20003
(202) 547-9292

IMPOTENCE

Impotence Institute of America
10400 Patuxent Pkwy, Ste. 485
Washington, DC 20006
(800) 669-1603

INCEST

Incest Survivors Resource Network International, Inc.
P.O. Box 7375
Las Cruces, NM 88006-7375
(505) 521-4260 (Hours: Monday–Saturday, 2–4 P.M. and 11 P.M.–Midnight,
Eastern time)

PET BEREAVEMENT

Bide-A-Wee Foundation
410 E. 38th St.
New York, NY 10016
(212) 532-6395

The Animal Medical Center
510 E. 62nd St.
New York, NY 10021
(212) 838-8100

Holistic Animal Consulting Center
29 Lyman Ave.
Staten Island, NY 10305
(718) 720-5548

RAPE/SEXUAL ISSUES

Austin Rape Crisis Center
1824 East Oltorf
Austin, TX 78741
(512) 440-7273

National Council on Sexual Addictions and Compulsivity
1090 S. Northchase Parkway, Suite 200
South Marietta, GA 30067
(770) 989-9754

Sexually Transmitted Disease Referral
(800) 227-8922

SMOKING ABUSE

Nicotine Anonymous
2118 Greenwich St.
San Francisco, CA 94123
(415) 750-0328

SPOUSAL ABUSE

National Coalition Against Domestic Violence
P.O. Box 34103
Washington, DC 20043-4103
(202) 544-7358

National Domestic Violence Hotline
(800) 799-SAFE

STRESS REDUCTION

The Biofeedback & Psychophysiology Clinic
The Menninger Clinic
P.O. Box 829
Topeka, KS 66601-0829
(913) 350-5000

New York Open Center
(In-depth workshops to invigorate the spirit)
83 Spring St.
New York, NY 10012
(212) 219-2527

Omega Institute
(A healing, spiritual retreat community)
260 Lake Dr.
Rhinebeck, NY 12572-3212
(914) 266-4444 (info)
(800) 944-1001 (to enroll)

Rise Institute
P.O. Box 2733
Petaluma, CA 94973
(707) 765-2758

The Stress Reduction Clinic
Center for Mindfulness
University of Massachusetts Medical Center
55 Lake Ave. North
Worcester, MA 01655
(508) 856-1616
(508) 856-2656

ABOUT THE AUTHOR

Carol Ritberger, Ph.D., is a medical intuitive and bioenergetic diagnostician. As a medical intuitive, she helps people understand how emotional, psychological, and spiritual energy can lie at the root cause of illness, disease, and life crises. As a bioenergetic diagnostician, she can literally "see" the human energy system, identifying where there are blockages that affect the wellness of the physical body.

An international speaker, Carol offers readings and workshops that focus on understanding how personality, stress, and emotions contribute to the formation of illness in the body. Her education includes personality behavioral psychology, and she holds a doctorate in theology.

Carol welcomes your letters, and she is available to teach workshops. However, she is unable to provide referrals for therapists, healers, or counseling services. Please contact her through the Hay House publicist or by e-mail: **cdraura@a.crl.com**

🦋 🦋 🦋

❦ ❦ ❦

We hope you enjoyed this Hay House book.
If you would like to receive a free catalog featuring additional
Hay House books and products, or if you would like information
about the Hay Foundation, please contact:

Hay House, Inc.
P.O. Box 5100
Carlsbad, CA 92018-5100

(760) 431-7695 or **(800) 654-5126**
(760) 431-6948 (fax) or **(800) 650-5115 (fax)**

Please visit the Hay House Website at: **www.hayhouse.com**

❦ ❦ ❦